This is the book I needed ......, first was diagnosed with anxiety. Packed with wisdom, practicality, and truth you can hang onto, this book will be one you reference often and recommend to others. J. D.'s story is a must-read for anyone who has ever battled with an anxious mind or wondered, "Where is God?" in the midst of their own mental storm.

Hannah Brencher
Author of *Fighting Forward* and *Come Matter Here*

J. D. Peabody offers a wise, kind, and deeply biblical understanding of what happens in the brain, body, heart, and soul of one who wrestles with anxiety. To be human is to fear. J. D. helps us understand and embrace how our body engages the process in a manner that will enable us to receive the presence of God as our comfort and ally.

Dan B. Allender, PhD
Professor of Counseling Psychology
The Seattle School of Theology and Psychology

This book is medicine to the soul—not just an important book but a very comforting and even paradigm-shifting book for all who think that God is on the side of winners. Christ is our armor! What better news can we have in our anxious lives?

Michael Horton
Westminster Seminary California, host of the White Horse Inn podcast and author of *Core Christianity*

I've been hearing sermons and studies on "putting on the whole armor of God" my whole life. But honestly, I've never known what it actually looked like to apply that idea to my everyday living. *Perfectly Suited* opened that door for me, and has given me an eminently practical, honest revelation on the topic. J. D.'s ability to transparently use his own mental health struggles as a backdrop helps him to use concepts and stories that for me, were at once both enormously encouraging and quietly convicting.

John Mays
Co-founder/Sr VP, Centricity Music

This book will be an excellent addition to the literature on Bible based treatment of anxiety disorders. Written by a man who knows its two subjects extremely well, the Bible and anxiety. Enthralling vivid descriptions of what it's like to suffer through and find ways out of obsessional fears.

Ian Osborn, MD
Author of *Can Christianity Cure Obsessive Compulsive Disorder?*

Perfectly Suited is an impeccable fit for anyone who's ever had a run-in with anxiety. J. D. Peabody encourages us to put on the armor of God not as a quick-fix for this mental, emotional, and spiritual challenge, but as part of a holistic, lifelong journey with Jesus—the one who walks beside us each step of the way.

Courtney Ellis
Author of *Happy Now* and *Uncluttered*

Author and pastor J. D. Peabody offers compassion, advice, and Biblical perspective to those who struggle with deep anxiety. Through honest reflections on his own struggles with OCD, Peabody becomes a beloved companion to all of us who find that our anxieties interfere with our relationship to God and our capacity to embrace God's infinite love for us.

Alice Fryling
Author of *Aging Faithfully: The Holy Invitation of Growing Older*

Jesus' grace is more than a proposition to be agreed with. It is meant to be lived out in freeing, healing ways. In *Perfectly Suited*, J. D. Peabody gives us a wonderful gift in this direction. Combining his ability to write engagingly with a disarming personal transparency, he takes us on a journey into the practical, life-giving implications of grace. Along the way he helps us to understand the strategic strength of our spiritual armor in whole new ways.

Dr. James Bradford
Lead Pastor, Central Assembly of God, Springfield, MO

PERFECTLY SUITED

THE ARMOR OF GOD
FOR THE ANXIOUS MIND

J. D. PEABODY

AspirePress

Perfectly Suited: The Armor of God for the Anxious Mind
© 2022 J. D. Peabody

Published by Aspire Press
An imprint of Tyndale House Ministries
Carol Stream, Illinois
www.hendricksonrose.com

ISBN: 978-1-4964-6594-8

Unless otherwise indicated, all Scripture quotations are taken from The Holy Bible, New International Version®, NIV® Copyright © 1973, 1978, 1984, 2011 by Biblica, Inc.® Used by permission of Zondervan. All rights reserved worldwide. www.zondervan.com The "NIV" and "New International Version" are trademarks registered in the United States Patent and Trademark Office by Biblica, Inc.

Scripture quotations marked MSG are taken from THE MESSAGE, copyright © 1993, 2002, 2018 by Eugene H. Peterson. Used by permission of NavPress. All rights reserved. Represented by Tyndale House Publishers, Inc.

Scripture quotations marked ESV are taken from the ESV® Bible (The Holy Bible, English Standard Version®). ESV® Text Edition: 2016. Copyright © 2001 by Crossway, a publishing ministry of Good News Publishers. The ESV® text has been reproduced in cooperation with and by permission of Good News Publishers. Unauthorized reproduction of this publication is prohibited. All rights reserved.

Book design by Cristalle Kishi

Portions of this book first appeared in the article "Praying for My Basal Ganglia" on Plough.com, February 8, 2021.

Excerpt from Psalm 108 is the author's translation; emphasis in Scripture quotations is the author's.

Excerpt from "Postludium" by Tomas Tranströmer, translated by Robin Fulton, from The Great Enigma, copyright ©2006 by Tomas Tranströmer. Translation © 2006 by Robin Fulton. Reprinted by permission of New Directions Publishing Corp. SALES TERRITORY: U.S., its territories and Canadian rights only. For British Commonwealth (excluding Canada) and Republic of Ireland rights: Tomas Tranströmer, New Collected Poems, translated by Robin Fulton (Bloodaxe Books, 2011). Reproduced with permission of Bloodaxe Book, www.bloodaxebooks.com

Library of Congress Cataloging-in-Publication Data

Names: Peabody, J. D., author.
Title: Perfectly suited : the armor of God for the anxious mind / by J.D. Peabody.
Description: Carol Stream, Illinois : Aspire Press, [2021] | Includes bibliographical references.
Identifiers: LCCN 2021049518 | ISBN 9781496465948
Subjects: LCSH: Anxiety--Religious aspects--Christianity. | Spiritual warfare.
Classification: LCC BV4908.5 .P38 2021 | DDC 241/.4--dc23/eng/20211130
LC record available at https://lccn.loc.gov/2021049518

Printed in the United States of America
010222VP

To Karin, my favorite person,

whose love and encouragement have

made this book (and so many other things) possible.

CONTENTS

INTRODUCTION

Come help us in this fight because
human "help" is worthless.

Psalm 108:12

've begun to think of writing as repentance.

I don't mean in some self-punishing, doing penance type of way. I'm not trying to pay for my wrongs through scribbling. I would probably run out of paper and ink.

But if it's true that the Greek word for repentance can mean "to turn around," then that's an appropriate description for my relationship to writing. It turns me around. The slow work of searching for words that are true shifts my gaze back to the Word who *is* Truth.

This book grew out of a series of Sunday morning messages I preached at New Day Church in Tacoma, Washington on the armor of God. I realize the world hasn't exactly been waiting for one more sermon series to be regurgitated in book form.

But I have been.

People often joke that pastors only work one hour a week. Not to whine, but I find that hour is about all I can take. The pace of weekly preaching is relentless. No sooner do you make and share a discovery than it's time to lay it down and move on to the next passage or topic. Your spiritual metabolism speeds up to the point where you can no longer absorb all the nutrients before a thought has already passed through the system.

I had delivered these sermons, but what I needed was the chance to spend more time with the material, to let my soul digest it. Because more than nearly any series I've preached, this one pressed against places I felt broken in a way that demanded more attention. I was dying for armor, and I didn't even realize it.

So, I write this for one very selfish reason: survival. This is a book about protection and vulnerability, about defensiveness and pain and avoidance. Mostly it's about grace—grace I have unknowingly resisted for a long time. Grace I am slowly gaining capacity to receive.

I pray that it serves to help you receive it, too.

ONE

MEET LEO

The courage to be is rooted in the God
who appears when God has disappeared
in the anxiety of doubt.

Paul Tillich

W hen our neighbors were the victims of an attempted break-in,
they decided it was time for a guard dog. So, they bought a
Doberman Pinscher puppy and named him Leo. We watched Leo
grow up, running around with little cones taped to his ears, training
them to stand fiercely at attention.

Leo has seen members of our family regularly enough to know
who we are. We live right next door. Our presence is an everyday
occurrence in his life. But anytime he hears us leave or arrive home,
he barks vigilantly as if we are dangerous intruders, as if we pose
a menacing threat to his existence. He can't seem to distinguish
between friend and foe. We always just say, "Hi, Leo," and walk past
his alarmed yapping.

I have named my brain Leo in his honor.

Since childhood, my conscience has had a high startle reflex, barking incessantly at me, often unnecessarily. I have frequently described it as a seared conscience, although I'm sure that's not how the Apostle Paul used the term. It just felt damaged in some way that made it hyper-vigilant.

A few years ago, things intensified. I found my head suddenly bombarded by a barrage of disturbing ideas and images that sent me into a tailspin. My mind raised the alarm at these thoughts that felt threatening and unstoppable, even when their only real power lay in my fear of them. I had no idea at the time that I was exhibiting the classic symptoms of someone with a full-blown clinical case of Obsessive Compulsive Disorder (OCD). Specifically, psychologists would categorize my experience as fitting in a subset of OCD known as scrupulosity. (But more on that later.)

The anxiety overwhelmed me. My response to the alarm was to try and tighten control of my mind. I circled my wagons and shrunk my world to avoid triggers—which only worsened the situation. Imagine noticing a leaky faucet, then cranking the knob so hard that it breaks off and water gushes out. The more I tried to rein in my mind, the stronger the torrent of thoughts became. This only increased my fears and made me try harder. It was a bewildering, corrosive cycle. And Leo barked ever louder.

Badly shaken, I went on a walk with my good friend, Bill, who just happens to be a therapist by profession. He listened graciously as the words and tears poured out. I tried unsuccessfully to make sense of what was happening. I was a terrified, jumpy wreck. When I ran out of words, in utter disbelief, I said emphatically, "I'm not an anxious person."

Bill laughed. Out loud.

Not the response I was going for. I wanted some comfort, some gentle reassurance that could bring me back to rationality. Instead, he laughed at my declaration that I wasn't anxious. He wasn't being mean; it was an involuntary, irrepressible reaction that seemed to say, "You're kidding, right? Have you even looked at yourself?"

That single laugh pulled me up short. I've always seen myself as an even-keel, unflappable type. And I took for granted I had a strong mind, with a firm grip on that mind at all times. This was not like me, was it? This fearful person battling unspeakable thoughts, this person who wanted to withdraw completely into a shell of avoidance—who was I?

One night, lying in bed, struggling against panic as my mind spun itself into another frenzy, I reached for the armor of God. I knew how Paul described it in his letter to the Ephesians:

Ephesians 6:10–17

Finally, be strong in the Lord and in his mighty power.
Put on the full armor of God, so that you can take your
stand against the devil's schemes. For our struggle is not
against flesh and blood, but against the rulers, against
the authorities, against the powers of this dark world and
against the spiritual forces of evil in the heavenly realms.

Therefore put on the full armor of God, so that when the
day of evil comes, you may be able to stand your ground,
and after you have done everything, to stand. Stand firm
then, with the belt of truth buckled around your waist,
with the breastplate of righteousness in place, and with

your feet fitted with the readiness that comes from the gospel of peace. In addition to all this, take up the shield of faith, with which you can extinguish all the flaming arrows of the evil one. Take the helmet of salvation and the sword of the Spirit, which is the word of God.

That night, I imagined myself hunkering down under the shield of faith. I cried out for protection against what felt like a volley of flaming arrows. I prayed intensely and passionately, invoking the Lord's covering. Surely this was spiritual warfare and the very setting for which I most needed the armor of God.

I'm not sure what I expected, but I didn't get it.

No peace that passeth understanding settled over me. The torment in my mind did not abate. I certainly didn't fall back to sleep the rest of the night. But as I have reflected on that experience and others since, I realize that I was up against a combination of misunderstandings.

For one thing, I didn't know myself as well as I thought. Emotionally, I was far more disconnected (and yes, anxious) than I realized and out of touch with my own needs. OCD simply put a new label to realities that had been lurking below the surface for decades. This meltdown that felt like a sharp break from the norm was not so far from where I had been living for a very long time. I simply reached a tipping point.

Beyond that, I discovered I had a very underdeveloped grasp of the armor of God. I was treating it more like magic, a secret power I could summon in a crisis and wait to be surrounded by an impenetrable shell. My prayer was childlike and desperate, which God thankfully hears regardless of theological savvy. But my limited vision of how he might answer could only leave me disappointed.

I share all this to give you a small, partial glimpse of what has led me to write this book. I don't know what has compelled you to pick it up. Perhaps you, too, are sensing a need for some armor. Maybe you feel exposed and embattled and are reaching for anything that might soothe and protect your frayed nerves. Maybe you're losing the fight and you need reinforcement. Or maybe the whole concept of the armor of God is new to you and you're just curious what I'm even talking about.

> I don't want to explain the armor of God—I want to wear it.

My hope is that this will not be an academic exercise. Thomas à Kempis once wrote that he would much rather *feel* guilt than be able to define it.[1] Well, I don't want to explain the armor of God—I want to wear it. As much as I value good scholarship, I'm less interested in analysis of the text in Ephesians than I am in connecting with one simple yet profound truth: I am in God's care.

What would it look like to live out of being loved by him? What would be different if I thoroughly trusted what he says he will do in terms of protecting me? I'll admit that is not my natural mindset. Yet nothing else reaches my deepest anxieties the way that truth does.

Back in 2012, Army Staff Sgt. Thalamus Lewis was serving in eastern Afghanistan. Along with the rest of the 41st Engineer

Company, he had just marched through a village when they came under heavy enemy fire.

Sgt. Lewis found himself knocked to the side of the road, ears ringing and head pounding. At the time, he was completely unaware that he had taken a bullet to the temple.

Incredibly, his Advanced Combat Helmet prevented the round from reaching his skull. The bullet entered his helmet on the right side. But the inner padding rerouted the bullet around the perimeter of his head and out the front of the helmet, completely protecting his brain from what would almost certainly have been a fatal shot.

In a special ceremony afterwards, Sgt. Lewis was presented with the remains of his helmet mounted on a plaque. He told reporters he used to resent all the protective gear he was required to wear. "I don't complain anymore," he said. "I'm a walking testament."[2]

A walking testament.

That's it, isn't it? I want to be living, breathing proof of all God has absorbed on my behalf. I'm not asking for a Damascus Road moment. I don't need drama and emotion or a mystical experience. I just want the truth I affirm intellectually to sink more deeply into the soil of my soul. Because most of the time I feel like I'm still trying to be the one protecting myself. I'm still squirming around in this armor when I want to be able to appreciate it and take full advantage of it.

Maybe none of us will grasp more than a fraction of grace this side of eternity. But if we can begin to catch glimpses of it, to receive it and even enjoy it, maybe we also can become walking testaments.

I have two hopes for this book. The first is that it will encourage you to see that although the armor of God may sound like something from another era, it's exactly what you need right now for whatever battle you're currently waging. Rather than being an abstract spiritual concept, it is crucial, practical truth for where you live.

My second hope is that you will see that the armor is not another Christian duty to perform and "get right." It's there to help you, not to add to the weight. I've lived most of my life focused (very earnestly) on my own valiant, well-intentioned efforts for God, and an inadequate grasp of God's armor has proved costly. I'd love it if my story can help unburden you in your journey.

FOR REFLECTION

1. Have you ever had someone give you feedback about yourself that was a surprise, but turned out to be true? How did that shape you?

2. What might be a way to practice receiving grace? What about that feels difficult or awkward?

3. What are you hoping to get out of reading this book?

TWO

A STRONGER STRONG

A good cry never hurt nobody.

Uncle Lumpy,
The Adventures of Little Orley

I still have the brown, imitation leather New American Standard Bible my parents gave me when I was in elementary school. On the front flyleaf, my boyish scrawl records a few key markers along my early spiritual path.

There is a brief note about rededicating my life to Christ . . . at the age of seven.

By the time I reached ten, I was no longer convinced my forgotten sinner's prayer from kindergarten had been adequate, so I re-rededicated my life and wrote it down in my Bible to be sure. That's followed by another entry memorializing the Sunday afternoon I prayed to be filled with the Holy Spirit (after feeling conscience-stricken for not going forward during the morning altar call at church).

I then jotted down this melodramatic gem when I returned from summer camp later that year: "Made Christ Lord, Master, Boss of my life. I am his slave."

I've shared those notes with friends, and the reaction I've gotten is, "How sweet!" Maybe a bit of a laugh at the adorability of such a spiritual fourth grader. But as I look back at my youthful self, I ache for that burdened boy, working so hard to make sure he got things just right for God. It turns out that my meltdown as a middle-aged man echoed the same concerns and misgivings I had felt back when I was ten.

I wanted to be a strong Christian. Most of the time, I just felt guilty. And uneasy.

Apparently, I'm not alone. I frequently have conversations with well-intentioned, believing people who are also full of striving and a vague insecurity. If blessed assurance is supposed to be the Christian's experience, something seems off.

Whenever we gather for corporate worship, we talk and sing about the wonders of God's amazing grace. We praise him for his ability to save and forgive us. Yet as we return to the everyday world, those concepts fade into the background. The available evidence suggests we don't place much confidence in grace when it comes to the most practical aspects of life. We're still relying heavily on our own defenses.

Such reluctance to trust is not without reason: our experiences and training conspire to tell us everything hangs on our own capacity to achieve our way to God. We've been shaped to consider grace as more of a backup quarterback who only gets called into play when things are especially dire for the team.

My point is not to critique, but as I've observed my own actions and those of others, an unsettling realization has emerged: *much of the activity we bill as Christian isn't generated by faith at all.*

A bold generalization, to be sure. But ask yourself: does trusting Christ produce the fear and anger so many Christians display toward the world he died to save? Does faith in the cross call for so many books and sermons promising some additional "secret" to a deeper life with God? Does belief that we are all equally in need of—and fully invited to—the table of grace generate the endless comparison and judgment found within church circles?

That is not to say our efforts at being good are insincere. In fact, the opposite is true. Large numbers of Christ-followers are driven by a genuine desire to be faithful servants. We live in the hope of pleasing God. We want him to smile and make his face shine upon us.

> We've been shaped to consider grace as more of a backup quarterback who only gets called into play when things are especially dire for the team.

But that's just it. We're not entirely sure he *is* satisfied. There is a bone-deep insecurity, no matter how strong of a show we're presenting to the world. Even those of us steeped in a lifetime of walking with Jesus don't always live as though we are counting on the fact that the Son within us perfectly pleases the Father already, let alone that God could truly find us lovable.

We default to dependence on our own striving. In short, we supplement Christ's work any way we can to shore up the ground beneath our feet.

During the Beijing Olympics of 2008, one TV report profiled an American athlete and her visit to an ancient Buddhist temple near the Olympic village. She herself wasn't religious, but she stopped to rub the belly of a Buddha statue on her way out, just for some pre-event good luck. She knew her athletic abilities were solid, but if there was a little extra boost of something that could tip fate her direction, she told the cameras she figured it couldn't hurt.

Such pragmatic superstition creeps into the way we think about the relationship between our deeds and God's blessing. And why would we think otherwise? We have so little context in life for unearned grace, so few relationships where we've encountered it firsthand. While we're grateful for the cross, we can barely conceive of what it represents. So we're not above tacking on some insurance, reinforcing our eternal standing with whatever might cover a few more bases, just for good measure.

Even still, we feel a bit precarious, because a nagging voice in the back of our heads reminds us that there's something in the Bible about how we all fall short. What if that is what's truest about us? We convince ourselves that in the end, what God cares about is that we're trying our best and that we want to be good. He's looking for effort and heart, isn't he?

So we put in the work and hope no one notices the cracks in our confidence. Meanwhile, the fear remains, driving all we do, keeping us vigilant, anxious, and exhausted.

If you had suggested this idea to me a few years ago—that my life was more performance than faith—I would have been offended. I love the gospel message, the profound beauty of God stepping in to resolve what was humanly impossible. Jesus offering us life through the counterintuitive move of his death. A comprehensive restoration generated entirely by holy love.

As a pastor, I've worked hard to keep my preaching centered on what Christ has done instead of a list of things we need to be doing. The very notion that I might be living an essentially proving-my-worth existence would have been too painful to consider, because it violates my core beliefs.

And yet.

Functionally, practically, realistically—we gravitate toward reliance on that self-generated struggle more than resting in God. Think about how you might finish the following sentences:

If I want God to bless me, I need to _____.

In order to experience closeness with Christ, I must _____.

If I am going to mature in my faith, that will require _____.

There are many possible answers. We would fill the blanks with good things: wholesome, productive, worthy things. And God certainly invites—even delights in—our participation in our own formation process. Entering into the work is part of the joy.

But if we're not careful, the way we complete those sentences can turn us into the primary actors and our accomplishments into the source of our acceptability. The scramble substitutes for faith.

I don't need to look any further than my own history to see evidence of this. Being a disciple of Jesus has normally revolved around a few key ideas for me:

MY DEFAULT DISCIPLESHIP WHEELHOUSE

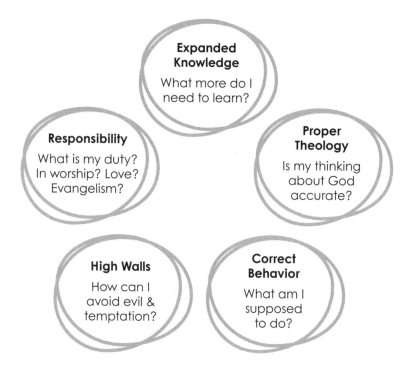

Expanded Knowledge
What more do I need to learn?

Responsibility
What is my duty? In worship? Love? Evangelism?

Proper Theology
Is my thinking about God accurate?

High Walls
How can I avoid evil & temptation?

Correct Behavior
What am I supposed to do?

Those all sound like worthwhile endeavors for any Christian to pursue. And yet I can talk at length about any of them without once mentioning anything Christ has done. They all revolve around expectations of myself.

> He never asks us to earn his love.

Back when I was attending seminary, theologian James Torrance came from Scotland as a visiting professor for one quarter. In his thick brogue, he would frequently remind our class, "The mandates of Scripture always flow from the indicatives of grace."

The language may be academic, but his point was essential (and often forgotten). Whatever God tells us to do stems from his compassion *that is already in place*. He never asks us to earn his love. And when we miss that, we miss the gospel.

This is not a rare form of confusion among churchgoers. A recent survey found that over half (52%) of Americans who consider themselves Christians believe that salvation can be attained by effort and being a good person.[3] That is a sobering and wide departure from the essence of faith.

If we are counting on anything we do, think, believe, know, feel, or experience to secure our standing with God, we're no longer living in grace. We're living in the imagined strength of striving. And that's not strong enough.

It's disturbingly easy for even the most seasoned, Bible-cherishing believers to end up there, and it can show up in the way we interpret

Scripture. Consider Paul's admonition in Ephesians, just before he launches into his description of the armor of God:

Ephesians 6:10
Finally, be strong in the Lord and in his mighty power.

Paul is speaking a word of encouragement, and I want greater strength in my life. I need it. But when I read that sentence through my flawed filters, the words, "Be strong," sound more like, "Man up." The verse takes on a chastening tone, telling me to pull myself together. It's the voice of a personal trainer who shows no mercy, shouting in my ear to be tough and dig deep and go for one more rep. Everything is depending on me.

> Strength lies within the ready reserves of God's storehouses, and he gladly offers to share it all.

I hear a series of *oughts*: "You *ought* to be stronger. You *ought* to be able to handle this better. You are not where you *ought* to be right now." What started out as an uplifting, life-giving statement gets twisted into a reminder that I'm not cutting it. And I respond by redoubling my efforts or retreating into a shame-filled corner.

But that's loading up Paul's words with meaning he never intended them to carry. A more precise translation of his phrase, "Be strong in the Lord" would be, "Strengthen yourselves in the Lord."

Strengthen yourselves. That conveys a decidedly different tone. That tells us strength is something we can find outside of us, a well we are invited to draw from rather than energy we manufacture. Strength lies within the ready reserves of God's storehouses, and he gladly offers to share it all.

In the book of 1 Samuel, the author tells the story of David using language that parallels Paul's:

1 Samuel 30:6b (ESV)
But David strengthened himself in the LORD his God.

This is remarkable, considering the context in which it happened. Before becoming king, David was being hunted by his predecessor, King Saul. For roughly eighteen months he lived under the protection of Israel's enemies, the Philistines. About six hundred fighting Israelite men and their families threw their lot in with David, and together they lived in the town of Ziklag.

Knowing the Philistines were planning to attack King Saul and his armies, David took his men and marched for three days to join them. But the Philistines doubted David's troops could be trusted battling their own countrymen, so they turned down the offer and sent them packing.

After making the three-day hike back to Ziklag, the men were met by a horrific sight. The Amalekites had attacked the village while the warriors were away, burning it to the ground and taking the women and children captive. It was more than the men could bear.

1 Samuel 30:4 (ESV)
Then David and the people who were with him lifted their voices and wept until there was no strength in them to weep.

What a raw, heart-wrenching scene. Hundreds of grown men crying their eyes out, inconsolable over the loss of their families. No one rushed to put a positive spin on the situation, spouting sunny takes such as, "At least there are no bodies!"

No one tried to minimize the pain by assigning meaning to the tragedy. It was just sad and awful and wrong. So, they cried. They cried until they didn't even have the energy to do that anymore. They were completely spent.

> Receiving empowerment from God goes hand in hand with realizing we've exhausted our own.

It is in this poignant moment that we're told David strengthened himself in the Lord. *When he didn't even have the strength to cry, he found strength in God.*

The timing is no coincidence. Receiving empowerment from God goes hand in hand with realizing we've exhausted our own.

As a rule, most of us prefer never reaching that point. We'd rather not feel the more difficult feelings. We don't like to admit how devastated we are, how hurt, how confused, how sad, how lonely, how inadequate, how scared. We invest tremendous amounts of energy denying the depth of those feelings, working very hard to appear strong against them.

We resist going there with everything we've got. We negotiate ways to keep life small enough to handle on our own. We cut ourselves off from God's incomparably great power because we are pouring all our effort into not needing it.

Philip Yancey once observed that grace, like water, flows to the lowest places.[4] If that's true, and I want to experience grace, I need to quit scrambling to reach high ground. It does me no good to distance myself from the true state of my heart, when if I admit just how low I am, the grace will flow down to meet me. God's best is most discoverable in our worst. His strength, he says, is made perfect in weakness.

And here's where my perception has needed to shift. In my mind, growing stronger in the faith equaled needing less grace. Becoming more self-sufficient. As I mature, shouldn't my struggle with sin diminish? Isn't it our goal to need the cross less and less the closer we get to eternity?

In a word, no. Scripture points the other direction, as does the experience of saints down through the centuries. Those we would consider from our vantage point to look the holiest and furthest along in faith are in fact the ones most humbled by their utter dependence on God for everything.

OLD VIEW OF GROWTH

Maturity = less need for cross

GOD'S VIEW OF GROWTH

Maturity = moving toward cross

The Bible says we are to grow *in* grace—not outgrow it. We lean in as redemption seeps ever further into hidden layers of our souls we never realized were aching for it. I've spent too many years straining to be sinless instead of learning what it means to live like a forgiven person.

To become stronger in faith is to own the reality of our "unstrong," to cry ourselves out (literally or metaphorically) and cling ever more tightly to the cross the longer we know Christ. It's all him. The life we now live we live by faith.

Faith. Banking entirely on what he has done. Entrusting ourselves more to what we can't see than to the things we can control. Living out of the belief that we are loved by a holy God.

David could have immediately led a search party into the desert. With a pack of angry men calling for blood (and his own emotions running high), it required enormous restraint to not jump into action. But he turned to God first, before making any move. He allowed the time he needed to lay his situation before God and wait for a response.

We have such a demanding internal drive to resolve our crises for ourselves. Circumstances make it feel urgent that we do so. I am learning to read my own urgency as the voice of my anxiety and an indicator that

I've spent too many years straining to be sinless instead of learning what it means to live like a forgiven person.

it's time to wait on God. Panic often masks itself as clarity, which gives good reason to pause. Staying in that tension—where we are desperate to act but choosing to wait and listen—is where we strengthen ourselves in the Lord.

FOR REFLECTION

1. Do you agree that much of what passes for Christian isn't generated by faith?

2. What have you relied on to make you feel better about your relationship with God?

3. How does living like you're forgiven look different from attempting to be sinless?

THREE

CONSCIENTIOUS OBJECTIONS

It is funny how mortals always picture us as putting things into their minds: in reality, our best work is done by keeping things out.

Screwtape,
The Screwtape Letters, C. S. Lewis

The universe is a difficult and dangerous place for a human. To live is to struggle. That is what you call an incontrovertible truth.

Being a Christian adds its own unique layer of burdens to the mix. "In this world, you will have trouble," the Lord told his friends (John 16:33).

That quote from Jesus still catches me off guard. I don't want to accept what he's saying. A stubborn idealism in my head wants to hang on to the notion that when lived properly, the Christian walk will safeguard me from life's most dire predicaments. If I'm doing things right, instinct tells me the hardships should decrease, not increase.

Yet from the days of the first disciples onward, placing your faith in Christ has meant stepping into an ongoing fight that is much larger than you—one you can't see, but at the same time can't avoid. We come to Christ for healing and forgiveness, only to find ourselves plunged into battle.

Paul writes as though armor is essential for every Christian, and armor implies we can expect danger to accompany our faith. He points out that the real adversaries we're up against can't be seen because they aren't other people (Ephesians 6:12). Peter backs him up, saying the devil himself is out prowling around, ready to pounce on our weaknesses (1 Peter 5:8). No matter how disturbing or unlikely we find the idea, Scripture claims an invisible reality presses in on the visible world, adamantly opposed to believers.

This raises the controversial, murky subject of spiritual warfare. Those two words generate vastly different reactions in the minds of Christians.

In one camp are those who dismiss the notion outright. These skeptics would say that what Paul called "forces of darkness" might be categorized today under labels such as clinical depression, some form of epilepsy, or even simple barometric pressure. With all the advances in psychology and biology, many would argue that there are natural explanations for things biblical authors attributed to demons and spirits (although Matthew 4:24 seems to suggest even they knew the difference between natural and spiritual maladies).

Critics of spiritual warfare raise theological objections as well. They would warn that morbid fascination with the demonic can distract from the truth of the gospel and the sufficiency of Christ. Best not to try too hard when it comes to peering into unseen realms.

At the other end of the spectrum are those who define every aspect of faith in terms of cosmic conflict. We are foot soldiers advancing with the angel armies against the kingdom of darkness. Any problem that arises is readily understood to be an attack of Satan, with demons lurking behind every tree.

This leads to framing our relationship with God in terms of battle strategy. If we're in a war, how do we win? Specific tactics are seen as essential to countering evil. Emphasis is often given to forcefulness in prayer, rebuking of evil spirits, and demonstrating unwavering belief in ultimate triumph. This creates a tremendous pressure to maintain adequate faith for the fight.

Such zeal can unwittingly give the devil far more credit and power than he deserves for challenges that are simply part of life. I think of the woman who once told my wife about her purchase of a new home. When she discovered rats in the basement, she took it as a sign of spiritual opposition to her move. Theoretically, I suppose Satan could have planned the infestation. But sometimes rats are just rats.

It's easy to fault people for their big reactions to spiritual warfare, but I can be equally as alarmist. At the height of my mental crisis, I struggled to make sense of what was happening in my mind. The possibility that my angst might have spiritual dimensions multiplied the anxiety. Was I sinning in some way and experiencing God's displeasure? One friend hinted ominously that I might be suffering demonic oppression. That suggestion hung over my subconscious like a black cloud, and it fed into my OCD's predisposition to scrape endlessly for explanations.

While all these discouraging thoughts swirled in my head, other voices argued that my suffering was due to mental illness, extreme stress, unresolved pain from childhood, or some sort of physical condition. The list of possibilities seemed endless.

At the end of the day, I could not definitively parse out what percentage of my struggle was instigated by a devilish adversary and what was due to something else. Like so many areas in life, when it came to spiritual warfare, I could only see through a glass darkly.

I didn't want to ignore possible dimensions to my pain, and at the same time I didn't want to scapegoat demons while overlooking more human factors in my story. And there was no way for me to say with any certainty whether my situation came about as the result of natural causes or something far more sinister.

But it didn't matter all that much.

Whatever the source, I was afflicted. It was troubling my soul, and I needed God's intervention. That meant that no matter what the cause, the required response was the same: reaching for his mercy. I didn't need full understanding as much as I needed rescue. I clung to Paul's reassurance that even if demons were at work, they couldn't alter God's love for me (Romans 8:38–39).

It is not my intention here to delve into arguments about the exact nature or extent of spiritual warfare. There are plenty of other, more qualified resources for exploring that topic. What the Bible and experience make clear for us on this front is that we do have foes. Those foes aren't always easy to identify, and we are vulnerable to their attacks.

We're vulnerable because we can't see the attacks coming. We're vulnerable because our sin-prone natures are susceptible to every hook the devil throws out there. We find most of his suggestions reasonable and attractive.

And we're vulnerable because we've already been hurt by friendly fire from other people trying to engage the enemy alongside us. We fight this battle with wounds and scars that weaken us.

In John's passage where Jesus speaks to his disciples about having trouble in this world, the Greek word for trouble refers to internal pressure. That certainly described my mental turmoil. No third party was needed to fan the flames of stress I felt inside.

In light of that, perhaps a more useful definition would be this:

> *Spiritual warfare is anything that negatively affects our spirits.*

What robs us of joy and peace? What fills us with worry or dread? What stirs up insecurity or anger? Potentially, such changes in us could be traced back to a direct assault by a celestial being. But most of the time, we're not preoccupied with protecting ourselves against demons; we're concerned about being hurt by people. Or letting ourselves down. Or not having enough. Or not being enough. Or how we are perceived.

Those are the possibilities that consume our attention and that can negatively affect our spirits. Once they're in play, the devil knows just how to exploit our worst anxieties. He may not always be the cause behind them, but he's ready to turn any and all of our struggles into spiritual battlegrounds. We can recognize his predictable methods:

SPIRITUAL WARFARE

ENEMY TACTICS

Deception	⟶	He's the father of lies who convinces us he's telling the truth. *(John 8:44)*
Temptation	⟶	He entices us with irresistible promises that prove hollow. *(Genesis 3:4-5)*
Confusion	⟶	He steals our clarity and introduces misunderstanding and doubt. *(Isaiah 41:28-29)*
Accusation	⟶	He undermines our confidence by shaming us with our guilt. *(Revelation 12:10)*
Fear	⟶	He fills us with worries that paralyze us. *(Matthew 13:22)*
Entrapment	⟶	He locks us in attachments and thought patterns we can't break. *(Proverbs 5:22)*
Discouragement	⟶	He tells us all the reasons why faith won't work. *(2 Corinthians 12:7)*
Conflict	⟶	He sows discord to isolate us from one another. *(2 Corinthians 2:10-11)*
Death	⟶	He kills off the good and introduces decay. *(John 10:10)*

Our enemy introduces these poisons through good times as well as bad. We equate difficulties with spiritual attacks, but even the devil knows that persecution often causes God's children to run straight into the arms of their Father. On the flip side, moments of success can prove fertile soil for darkness when we lose sight of God's role in creating them.

Fortunately, God offers us protection that is effective in all circumstances. When Paul refers to the full armor of God, he uses the word *panoplia*, which is where we get our English word panoply. It means "a complete set." God offers us head-to-toe coverage that is thoroughly effective, no matter what the struggle.

SPIRITUAL WARFARE

ENEMY TACTICS MET BY CHRIST

Deception	➤——➤	He is Truth. *(John 1:14)*
Temptation	➤——➤	He is Fulfillment. *(Philippians 4:19)*
Confusion	➤——➤	He is the Way. *(John 14:6)*
Accusation	➤——➤	He is our Advocate. *(Romans 8:34)*
Fear	➤——➤	He is Love. *(John 15:13)*
Entrapment	➤——➤	He is Freedom. *(John 8:36)*
Discouragement	➤——➤	He is Hope. *(Colossians 1:27)*
Conflict	➤——➤	He is Peace. *(Ephesians 2:14)*
Death	➤——➤	He is Life. *(John 1:4)*

These are not worn out, over-simplified slogans about Christ, drained of any actual meaning. They are incredible realities that grow larger the further they are explored.

Some people attempt to use the promise of Christ's total protection as a way of spiritual bypassing to avoid dealing with pain or facing their own hearts directly. If you claim the victory in Jesus, they reason, then there's no need to go digging up the past or reflecting too much on failures. The old has gone; the new has come. Forget those things you'd rather not remember. Believe and be healed. It's all under the blood.

> I am finding that some of the hardest work is remaining on the battlefield.

But here's the thing: Paul wouldn't suggest we need armor if there wasn't still fighting to be done. Christ's total, decisive win on the cross doesn't eliminate our battles—it empowers us to engage the enemy without fear and to face ourselves honestly. When we enlist God's protection, the nature of the fight changes, but it doesn't go away.

John Bunyan called believing, "sweating work." He once wrote, "He that undertakes to believe, sets upon the hardest task that ever was proposed to man . . ."[5] We have hard, courageous, sweating work to do.

I am finding that some of the hardest work is remaining on the battlefield. In those moments when my anxieties are wild-eyed in the face of my fears, I want to bolt. I want to deny the fear and reassure myself things aren't that bad. I want to get out through whatever exit is closest.

Spiritual warfare requires us to sit still with what overwhelms us, trusting that God will give us the strength to wait, and that ultimately he will come and fight for us.

If we stay at our post, what we discover is that we can do more than just survive the ordeal. Endurance, as James puts it, pays off. God turns our worst fears into a creative opportunity. Dread becomes one more instrument in his hands for growing our faith and expanding our souls.

Søren Kierkegaard put it this way:

> The man who, holding fast to God, remains with the dread which obedience involves, does not allow himself to be "deceived by its countless counterfeits." Then at last the attacks of dread, though they are fearful, are not such that he flees from them. For him dread becomes a serviceable spirit which against its will leads him whither he would go. Then when it announces itself, when it craftily insinuates that it has invented a new instrument of torture far more terrible than anything employed before, he does not recoil, still less does he attempt to hold it off with clamour and noise, but he bids it welcome, he hails it solemnly . . . he shuts himself up with it; he says, as a patient says to the surgeon when a painful operation is about to begin, "Now I am ready." Then dread enters his soul and searches it thoroughly, constraining out of him all the finite and the petty, and leading him hence whither he would go.[6]

Sounds like an awful idea to me. Where is the appeal in locking myself in a room with my worst nightmares? How can I calmly accept what makes me recoil in terror or disgust? I'd rather keep thinking of spiritual warfare in more other-worldly terms that don't demand such a confrontation with reality. And I'm not even sure I know how to "welcome my dread" for any length of time.

> When we press into the center of our greatest dread, we find our Savior arrived there first.

Yet this is Calvary, where Jesus chose to drink the very cup that made him sorrowful unto death. This is the cross, where Christ remained to the end, even though it was within his power to come down. When we press into the center of our greatest dread, we find our Savior arrived there first.

I do not wish to go there. Ever. But I do want to operate more out of trust. And I can see how this way of engaging the enemy leaves me no choice but to trust God.

We may never comprehend the full dimensions of this war in which we find ourselves. The point is that we're not alone in it. Christ stands with us, flanking us on all sides with his undeniable, resurrected self.

FOR REFLECTION

1. What do you think of the definition that spiritual warfare is anything that negatively affects our spirits?

2. Do you tend to dismiss the idea that there are spiritual forces at play in the world, or do you go the other direction and interpret everything as spiritual?

3. Out of the list of enemy tactics, which do you find the most prevalent in your life? How have you seen Christ counter those attacks?

FOUR

THE ARMOR OF ME

I walk slowly into myself,
through a forest of empty suits of armor.

Tomas Tranströmer, *Postludium*

When my older sister was still a toddler, my mother went away for the weekend to a women's retreat, leaving my father in charge of his little girl for the first time. Parenting a daughter was new, and in an era when most men had little training in childcare, it's no small miracle they both survived those few days together. But when the women arrived back at the church after their weekend away, my mother was greeted by an unforgettable sight: my sister in a Sunday dress, which my father had managed to put on her both backwards *and* inside out.

Part of the reason God's armor has felt unwieldy to me may lie in the fact that I've been attempting to wear it the wrong way. What if my understanding of how it works has been flipped in my mind? Can I turn it right side out again to function more like it was intended?

The vocabulary of the armor of God is not foreign to me. I was surrounded by it as a child. Our church sang songs with lyrics such as these:

Onward, Christian soldiers, marching as to war . . .
Stand up, stand up for Jesus, ye soldiers of the cross . . .

I may never march in the infantry, ride in the cavalry,
shoot the artillery,
I may never fly o'er the enemy,
but I'm in the Lord's army . . .

I don't know how many Sunday School lessons and Bible studies and camp talks and flannelgraphs and sermons I sat through where I learned the various pieces of the armor of God and their counterparts in Roman military attire. The concept became ingrained in my Christian consciousness.

Still, there was a sense in which all the meticulous attention to details of the armor failed to bring it home. My third-grade mind didn't even try to comprehend what it meant to say I was in the Lord's army. I just liked the hand motions that went with the song.

The only real takeaway I internalized from all that exposure to the armor concept was that it was my responsibility to pick it up and put it on. If I could follow all the guidelines laid out in Ephesians, then I would have the protection I needed. In other words, as I saw it, *my actions were my armor.*

Underneath the spiritualized language, I was counting on personal devotion as my security, rather than anything God might provide.

This turns discipleship into what P. T. Forsyth referred to as, "Christian correctitude."[7]

And here lies the problem. We end up reading our Bibles to find out what we are supposed to do, rather than to center ourselves around the surpassing greatness of what Christ has already done. Our sermons and studies become burdensome lectures because we focus on what is being asked of us rather than on what has been given to us. We concentrate on the picking up and putting on instead of the armor itself.

We've dressed ourselves backwards and inside out.

When Paul admonished the church in Ephesus to "put on" the full armor of God, the Greek word he chose also describes "sinking into" a garment. Picture easing yourself down onto a soft couch or wrapping yourself in a thick blanket. To sink into something is effortless, more allowing it to happen than striving to attain it.

Could we sink into God's armor? I like the imagery. Is it possible?

In his book exploring OCD and faith, Dr. Ian Osborn shares the story of Thérèse of Lisieux.[8] Thérèse was born in the late nineteenth century. She was about as thoroughly religious as someone can be. She received her education in a Benedictine school, then went on to become a Carmelite nun. Carmelites maintain a very strict lifestyle, praying for long hours every day, enduring very ascetic conditions and observing complete silence for extended periods. If anybody exemplified diligently working to put on their own armor, it was Thérèse.

Despite her devotion, uncontrollable doubts and fears haunted her. She tried performing severe acts of self-punishment to counter what was happening in her mind, but the effort provided no comfort to her conscience.

Unable to find any method of alleviating her mental distress, Thérèse concluded she needed a fundamentally different approach to God. After much prayer and reflection on Scripture, she developed what she came to call "The Little Way."

It was a radical departure from the rigid moralism of her time. She focused on all the verses that portray God caring for the small and humble—verses like these:

> "Let the little children come to me." (Matthew 19:14)

> "As a father has compassion on his children, so the Lord has compassion on those who fear him." (Psalm 103:13)

> "I tell you the truth, unless you change and become like little children, you will never enter the kingdom of God." (Matthew 18:3)

Thérèse concluded that God's primary request of her was to remember her own smallness. Rather than cultivate self-sufficiency, she sought to adopt the attitude of a young child relying on a parent for everything: or in other words, "I will have the right of doing stupid things up until my death if I am humble and if I remain little!"[9]

Initially, the Little Way sounds as if it goes against everything young Christians are taught about healthy discipleship. Scripture admonishes us to "grow up in all things" and to not be "infants tossed back and forth." Where does maturity come into play if we are staying small?

I have a second Bible from my youth, one I purchased for myself when I was in middle school. I underlined a number of verses during those formative years of adolescence. Flipping through the pages now, I see a common thread in the passages I singled out. They are predominantly calls to action, the instructional sections that mapped out an identifiable way for me to feel I was doing enough to satisfy God.

One of my greatest recurring anxieties is the possibility that I might in some way not be taking my sin seriously enough. That sounds ultra-spiritual, but it is more fear-driven than pious. I review not just my actions but every internal agenda, and I come to the same conclusion as Jeremiah: the heart is a convoluted mess. I scrape my mind for any residue of wrong that might need to be confessed and eradicated, only to discover new twisted layers underneath. Pulling the lid off of my soul felt like staring into a bottomless cauldron of horrors.

> The alternative to being responsible is not being irresponsible—it is trusting God with the responsibility, the way a child trusts a parent with their care.

It never occurs to me in the midst of all the soul scrubbing that perhaps part of what God desires for me is freedom from the self-loathing and cruel harshness that tries to pass itself off as making me more like him. The very self-admonishment I equate with holiness is in fact distorting my perception of God.

I am learning there is a great difference between obedience and compulsion. Pursuing the path of taking "full responsibility" for my sin only pushes me toward despair, because I find that the problem is deeper and more pervasive in me than I can begin to address. I am unable to discern my true motivations with certainty. The more I dissect my confessions, the less adequate they seem, pulling me further down the rabbit hole of introspection.

My attempts to fully own my sin end up competing with my ability to accept what Christ did on my behalf. He went to the cross precisely *because* we are all incapable of taking full responsibility for our own sin.

Martin Luther addressed the fallacy of such thinking. "This attitude springs from a false conception of sin, the conception that sin is a small matter, easily taken care of by good works; that we must present ourselves unto God with a good conscience; that we must feel no sin before we may feel that Christ was given for our sins."[10]

The alternative to being responsible is not being irresponsible—it is trusting God with the responsibility, the way a child trusts a parent with their care. That's the Little Way.

Thérèse's point was not to encourage us to stay stuck in some kind of stunted development, but to remain in a state of total dependence. Rather than working hard to move past the need for more grace, we embrace our perpetual reliance on it.

What does staying small look like? Author Pia Mellody identified five essential characteristics that describe the natural state of a child.[11]

THE NATURAL STATE OF A CHILD

Valuable	Every child has inherent worth.
Vulnerable	Children need care and protection.
Imperfect	Learning and making mistakes are part of growing up.
Dependent	Children should not need to fend for themselves.
Immature	Expectations need to be age appropriate.

All these characteristics translate equally well to describe what it looks like to live as God's children. Do we believe we are of great value to him? Can we acknowledge and accept our vulnerability? Could we allow our imperfection? What about choosing to count on God instead of feverishly attempting to measure up? And are we able to show grace to ourselves, knowing our faith is still developing and we do not yet see what we will become?

It was C. S. Lewis who said, "When I became a man, I put away childish things, including the fear of childishness and the desire to be very grown up."[12]

Spiritual maturity never means independence. And God does not call us to count on our own self-protection. Instead, he offers us something completely different. Isaiah tells us this:

Isaiah 59:15b–17a
The LORD looked and was displeased
that there was no justice.
He saw that there was no one,

he was appalled that there was no one to intervene;
so his own arm worked salvation for him,
and his own righteousness sustained him.
He put on righteousness as his breastplate,
and the helmet of salvation on his head . . .

Here, the armor of God is worn by none other than God himself. He puts it on to bring the salvation nobody else could make happen. It is rescue. It is powerful. It is swift and sure. *The armor represents God's action on our behalf.*

This way of looking at it changes everything. It means when we take up (or sink into) the armor of God, we are not simply grabbing a resource he has put at our disposal to grow our own righteousness. We are letting God outfit us with what he's done for us. We are choosing to stay small and rely solely on his efforts for our defense.

Easier said than done.

In the epic story of David and Goliath, King Saul attempts to outfit the young David with a complete set of royal combat gear—helmet, armor, and sword (1 Samuel 17:38). Understandably, the king is worried about sending the inexperienced youth out against a formidable enemy with no protection.

But the armor he provides is heavy and ill-fitting. You can picture David awkwardly trying to move about as he wears it, clanking around until he finally gives up in frustration.

1 Samuel 17:39b
"I cannot go in these," he said to Saul,

"because I am not used to them."
So he took them off.

David decides to throw safety to the wind and forego the sensible precautions. That ended up being exactly the right choice, since his protection lay elsewhere. It would have been impossible for him to run toward the showdown while winding his sling if he was hampered by Saul's security uniform.

Sometimes I act as though I am doing what David did, turning down God's offer of protection and going out to slay giants on my own. I haven't worn God's armor much, so it doesn't feel natural. But the analogy breaks down, because it is God's help I'm refusing, not Saul's. I'd rather grab what I know and find comfortable. And I have multiple options I go to regularly when I am in self-preservation mode. I call it the Armor of Me:

THE ARMOR OF ME

The Belt of Denial	Problem? What problem?
The Breastplate of Humor	It won't hurt as much if I make a joke.
Feet Ready with a Plan of Escape	I'm just going to check out for a while.
The Shield of Perfectionism	If I get this one thing right . . .
The Helmet of Avoidance	Less exposure equals less pain.
The Sword of Blame	At least it's not my fault.

My armor has many additional elements God's doesn't offer, such as the shoulder pads of delusion, the face mask of people-pleasing, and the shin guards of distraction. I've got plenty of choices, and I slip into them without even thinking.

Psychologists would refer to these components as *feelings defenses*—ways of shielding ourselves from the pain of difficult emotions. And in times of trauma, they prove incredibly valuable. Feelings defenses are a God-given measure of safety and relief when the world is unbearable.

We pick them up when we are very young, and they become so ingrained in our responses that they are almost instinctual. A threat appears, and immediately our defenses are right there to meet it.

But over time, they outstay their usefulness. We begin to live in them permanently. They start to shape our choices regardless of the situation. That's when they become armor, a second skin we never shed. The humor that served well to break tension during a quarrel now stands in the way when anyone tries to get close. The "happy place" in your mind that got you through a crisis soon occupies all your thoughts and makes real life look even more miserable. The perfectionism that rewarded you with a job well done turns into an unrelenting, daily taskmaster.

The more I looked inward, the more I realized what a constant state of self-protection I occupied. I didn't even know what it felt like to be without my armor. That recognition made me conscious of how heavy it is, how much my own armor weighs me down. And I am weary of it.

If I'm going to wear the armor of God, I first need to remove the Armor of Me. I can't hold the shield of perfectionism and the shield of faith at the same time. The belt of truth won't fit if I'm wrapped in denial.

I have been trying to wear both, to supplement God's armor with a secondary layer of protection. I thought it was helping, and instead it is just in the way. That means unlearning patterns that have become second nature.

Dr. Henry Cloud and Dr. John Townsend once wrote, "We change our behavior when the pain of staying the same becomes greater than the pain of changing."[13]

On the playground at my elementary school, the classic swinging rings always offered a challenge. You could jump up and grab the first ring, then cross from one to the next until you reached the other end. But to move across, you had to let go of one ring as you reached for one further along. There was a moment of trust required as you released what had been keeping you aloft and swung your arm through the air to hold on to something new.

To return to the "Little Way" of Thérèse, staying small means there is a moment of trust required as we let go of the defense systems we've adopted to feel safe and avoid overwhelming feelings. We hand responsibility for our well-being back to God, our good and loving Father.

What we discover is that he's far better at doing his job than we are.

Once I became aware of all these defenses I was using, I started after them with a vengeance. Removing the Armor of Me became my all-consuming mission.

This quickly took me to a place of self-loathing, because I discovered just how tightly I had wrapped my armor around me and how difficult it was to step out of it. I became highly frustrated and ashamed over my lack of progress. The anxiety over attempting to change intensified. I felt this huge responsibility to fix myself, and I couldn't do it.

I shared this state I was in with my friend Bill. "I'm trying to knock down these defenses," I confessed, "but I can't do it."

Once again, his response surprised me. "Maybe you don't need to."

He went on to suggest I redirect my energies toward curiosity. Maybe instead of shutting down, I could invite God to help me ask questions. What was generating my fears? What was sending my very being into so much panic? If I could identify and care for those places, my self-protection mechanisms might begin dissolving on their own. My mind and body would no longer need to be on constant high alert because the perceived threat would no longer feel as threatening.

Save guilt for sin.

Working hard to peel off my armor was becoming one more manifestation of my compulsive scraping. I was laboring mightily to make myself better on my own. And the attempt to speed my healing was becoming one more place where my harsh inner critic was having a heyday.

The moral? *Save guilt for sin.* We're not called to live in a state of constant recrimination and shame. As you become aware of former blind spots and areas for growth, be kind to yourself in the process of change. You picked up your defenses because you felt vulnerable; laying them back down will leave you feeling exposed. An all-out frontal assault on your own armor may not be the best way to approach change.

It all needs time. A friend of mine who struggles with alcoholism once described the journey to recovery as "ten miles in, ten miles out." We cannot rush through what is a lifelong process.

And our need for help changing becomes one more opportunity to stay small. We can entrust the work of being transformed to God, letting Jesus replace our backward, inside-out armor with his garments of praise.

FOR REFLECTION

1. In your experience of Christianity, have you seen more emphasis placed on what God is asking of his followers, or what he has given us?

2. What do you imagine "staying small" might look like in your own life? What about that feels foreign?

3. What piece of your own armor would you most like to lay down?

FIVE

TRUTH THAT SURROUNDS

To be nobody-but-yourself—in a world which
is doing its best, night and day, to make you
everybody else—means to fight the hardest
battle which any human being can fight;
and never stop fighting.

e. e. cummings

recall owning two belts when I was a boy. One was army green
with a military style, flip-top roller buckle. It projected the right
image when I pretended to be G. I. Joe, but I could never quite make
that fastener work. The other belt was more suited to some rodeo
circuit out West, with an ornate silver buckle on one end of the strap
and a pointy metal tip on the other.

In both cases, the hardware is what made them memorable. The
belts themselves were nothing to write home about. Most belts
aren't: usually a thin band of leather, fabric, or even just rope. Hardly
what you would call substantial.

Not much has changed in two millennia. The belts worn by Roman
soldiers back in Paul's time were comparable to the type we would

wear today. And the belt was arguably the least compelling part of their armor. Helmets and shields gleam brighter in our imaginations. Even the shoes hold more fascination than a belt.

So, it is worth pondering why the Apostle Paul would start out his description of the armor of God with the belt of truth. The one flimsy piece of clothing we'd hesitate to even classify as armor gets the distinction of being first in the list.

Perhaps the answer can be found in its function rather than its substance—because a belt is what it does. It shapes. It defines. It gathers in. It holds everything together. It sets our outer limits and encircles us.

I grew up in a home where the belt of truth was cinched up tight. My parents placed a high value on Scripture, which served as the lens through which all truth claims were evaluated. As a result, to my young eyes, reality looked crystal clear. On any given topic, if I wanted to discover truth, I need only examine what God had communicated in the pages of the Bible, and that would be that.

Imagine my surprise to discover that the world at large did not share the same deference to Scripture. Whatever widespread cultural respect the Good Book may have once enjoyed evaporated long ago. Not only does the general population treat the Bible as inconsequential—even many Christians question its veracity and (let's be real here) rarely read much of it or know what it says.

To complicate matters even further, I learned I needed to be wary of believers proclaiming their undying commitment to truth. Different Christians can have widely varying ideas as to what that truth is. We're all largely blind to our own biases. Holding fast to Scripture and holding fast to a favorite interpretation of Scripture can be very different things.

In this present era, promoting the idea of any absolute truth strikes many people as arrogance and absurdity. No one cares to hear whatever proofs you might offer to back your truth claim. Everything is seen as a matter of perspective that can be refuted by equally compelling evidence for an alternate stance. There's not much interest in getting to the truth, because truth, it seems, can be whatever you make of it, and all opinions are treated as equally valid. Skepticism abounds.

> If Paul is correct to include truth as part of the armor of God, in a very real sense we don't defend truth—it defends us.

Of course, this creates a bind for followers of Jesus. Christianity has always staked everything on the gospel being true. If truth as a concept is irrelevant, then Christ himself is irrelevant, because he made the staggering claim to BE the truth (John 14:6).

That dilemma prompts us to set about doing our best to defend truth and preserve it. We break out the books on apologetics and outline the logic of belief. We pile up the sandbags, hoping to stave off the wave of false teaching that has reached flood stage. And we worry that sound doctrine is being lost forever.

No doubt there are grounds for concern, and as believers, we are called to vigilance. But if Paul is correct to include truth as part of the armor of God, in a very real sense we don't defend truth—it defends us.

It's not our job to protect God. Zeal to defend his truth often exposes a lack of faith that the Lord can take care of himself.

No one would dispute the need to watch our theology closely. But it requires a certain humility often lacking in church leadership. When we are convinced we are the sole guardians of truth, we operate in the name of Christ while often acting completely at odds with the character and purpose of Christ. As Chaim Potok has noted, "There are times when those who fear God make themselves very unpleasant as human beings."[14]

Rather than attempting to stand up for truth, what would it look like if we lived as though truth were standing up for us?

Noble as such an idea might sound, it's a tough sell in real life. Truth regularly feels unsafe, as though it is on a mission to expose us. Why on earth would we turn to it for protection? If all it will do is tell us what we don't want to hear, we would rather cast aside the belt and find our safety elsewhere.

In the book of Isaiah, God's people were doing exactly that. He confronted them about their choice, saying,

Isaiah 28:15
You boast,
"We have entered into a covenant with death,
with the realm of the dead we have made an
agreement.

When an overwhelming scourge sweeps by,
it cannot touch us,
for we have made a lie our refuge
and falsehood our hiding place."

In this verse, the people of God weren't being attacked by falsehood; they were running to it. They were willfully preferring it. Lies had become their go-to defense against disaster.

The Israelites were not unique in that regard. Several years ago, researchers conducted an experiment in which they captured video of people engaged in casual conversations, meeting strangers for the first time. In the majority of cases, *participants lied two or three times within a ten-minute conversation.*[15] In the stressful context of engaging with unfamiliar faces, keeping up a façade feels safer.

In a separate study, social scientists explored lying habits in multiple countries around the world. Geography and culture turned out to make no difference in how frequently people fabricate when they talk. The final report stated it plainly: "These findings suggest that individuals around the world are similarly dishonest at their core."[16]

Christians are not immune to such tendencies. We are all routinely drawn toward making lies our refuge and falsehood our hiding place. And given the nature of deception, we're not always even aware of what we're doing.

Some of us buy into the fiction that there is no inherent conflict between faith and the spirit of the age. We'd rather serve Christ in a way that fits indistinguishably with our surroundings. So we convince ourselves that discipleship doesn't have to put us at odds with the world.

For others, the trend lines of postmodernity alarm and grieve us, and we run for the shelter of denial. We hide behind the lie that we can make unwanted circumstances less real through retreat or resistance.

As a pastor, there have been times when I have not known how to speak into a current issue or event. I become paralyzed. Fear of saying the wrong thing has prevented me from saying anything. Instead of acknowledging that fear, I have comforted myself with the self-congratulatory delusion that I "stick to the main thing" in my preaching, all while failing to equip the congregation to navigate life's most complex problems.

We all turn to whatever will fend off pain and anxiety. Lies simply make us feel better. Here are a few examples of common untruths that we think will protect us:

LIES OF REFUGE

I can understand my way out of my problem.

If I keep busy I won't have to face the pain.

Isolating prevents shame.

I can perform my way into grace.

I can fill the void inside with possessions and distraction.

Talking about a problem will make it worse.

Lying itself is a kindness.

Because these are deceptions, the refuge they provide is also an illusion. Any safety we are counting on eventually crumbles away and leaves us exposed.

God could see through the falsehoods that had captivated Israel. He knew they would not last, and he offered his people a greater truth:

Isaiah 28:16–17

So this is what the Sovereign Lord says:
"See, I lay a stone in Zion, a tested stone,
a precious cornerstone for a sure foundation;
the one who relies on it
will never be stricken with panic.
I will make justice the measuring line
and righteousness the plumb line;
hail will sweep away your refuge, the lie,
and water will overflow your hiding place . . ."

When calamity strikes, God says, all that misplaced trust is going to come crashing down. Everything that felt so secure and safe will disintegrate before our eyes. All we can count on in the end will be the bedrock provided by God himself.

It is no coincidence that Peter identifies these verses with Jesus (1 Peter 2:6). He is our Rock, our Sure Thing that will offer shelter in the fiercest storm. All other ground, as the old hymn observed, is sinking sand.

If we reflect on what it means to say Jesus is the embodiment of truth, we can begin to catch a glimpse of how he acts as our armor. It is the gospel itself—the Son of God living, dying, and rising again—that offers us protection worthy of our trust.

GOSPEL TRUTH SAYS...

God loves me.

God understands the human condition.

God knows grief and pain.

God is still offering rest to the weary.

Life is more than what we see.

There is hope.

Christ will come back for us.

I am forgiven.

Nothing can separate me from him.

He is with me in my struggles.

I can count on him.

In many contexts, when we speak of truth, we're referring to facts. The word fact comes from the Latin word *factum*, which means *something done*. That definition echoes Christ's words from the Cross when he declared, "It is finished."

The reconciling work of his death became the ultimate Something Done, the fact that sets us free from fear of rejection and condemnation by God. The good news of Jesus protects us from misconceptions about God that would have us believe he could never accept us.

But the gospel doesn't stop at forgiveness for the wrongs we've done—it speaks to the wrongs we've endured. In Jesus, we find the truth of God caring for the weak and wounded and oppressed. Psychiatrist Frank Lake said, "He reconciles to God by His Cross not only sinners, but sufferers. Not only the memories of culpable sin which condemn the conscience, but the deeper memories of intolerable affliction which condemn faith as a delusion, these too are confronted by the fact of Christ's cross."[17]

The Crucifixion reaches beyond our pardon to overcome every last bit of sin's devastation in the world. God cares about the brokenness and not just the guilt. The Christ who bore our iniquities is also the Savior who took up our infirmities and sorrows.

As my OCD escalated, unwanted, nonsensical ideas invaded my brain. They felt decidedly out of character, shocking, or shameful. Psychologists call these thoughts *ego-dystonic* because they run contrary to a person's core identity. Their very existence proved distressing, and their persistence caused me to wonder if maybe they really *did* represent me on some level.

> God cares about the brokenness and not just the guilt.

Then a new layer of panic arose: what if I couldn't ever purge them from my head? If you've ever tried to outrun your brain, you know how counterproductive (and frightening) that is. My mind made a point of proving it could generate an endless flow of alarming triggers.

To combat the chaos inside, I retreated to the lies that: 1.) Returning to the way my mind used to function is all it would take to make me feel better; 2.) Ruminating on the thoughts would bring clarity; and 3.) Working diligently to figure myself out would ultimately succeed.

But the more I tried, the less confident I became in separating the true from the false. Even when I could logically see the absurdity, I found myself compelled to try to understand and block each metastasizing thought, which led to deep despair.

Nobel Prize winner Ralph Bunche once said, "If you want to get across an idea, wrap it up in a person."[18] My wife became the person God used most often to wrap up his truth for me in my bleakest moments. She listened compassionately (and repeatedly) to my fears and my doubts without being dismissive or judgmental. Then she would smile, look me in the eyes, and say, "I'm not afraid of your thoughts. I know who you are."

Her response ushered in a level of relief almost too sacred to reduce into words. It reconnected me with this: I was known and loved by someone grounded in reality, someone who recognized the lies for what they were, and was not intimidated by them. The grace of God flowed through her and reached recesses inside me that had been walled off from its light. She handed me the belt of truth to gird me back up, and that truth offered the sanctuary my hounded soul craved.

And she showed me in the most tangible way what it means for Jesus to say he is the truth. There is a personal, relational dimension to it. Truth isn't merely a statement to be affirmed or a doctrine to be championed. Truth has a will that searches us out. Jesus is not afraid of your untruths. He knows you, and he knows himself. He looks for where we have been taken captive by "fine-sounding arguments," not to shame, but to protect.

And then, once again, he hems us in on all sides as he shows us the scars that speak the greatest truth of all: we are loved by a holy God who has done the utmost to make us his own.

What an unassailable defense.

FOR REFLECTION

1. Can you think of an occasion where truth protected you? What did that look like?

2. Looking at the "Lies of Refuge" list, is there one that resonates for you? What would you add to the list?

3. Write out some truths you know about Christ. What is one that you feel has been a safeguard? Take a moment and thank God for it.

SIX

THE SECOND LIST LIFE

It wasn't that the Gospel proved useful for
my many worries but that the Gospel
proved the uselessness of my worries and
so refocused my whole attention.

Henri Nouwen, *Here and Now: Living in the Spirit*

As he delves into his discussion of the armor, Paul moves directly from the component that provides the least physical coverage—the belt—to that which provides the most: the breastplate. Yet he gives this larger piece only the briefest mention without elaborating on what he means by a "breastplate of righteousness." All we're told is that we're to wear it (Ephesians 6:14).

It could be that Paul never dreamed we would subject his armor analogy to such meticulous scrutiny. He may have been thinking more holistically, seeing no need to imbue every detail with hidden meaning. There's always a danger of reading too much into individual words.

On the other hand, Paul's brevity here might also suggest he expected his readers to be so familiar with the imagery that no further explanation was needed. They could extrapolate on the theme for themselves. After all, the value of armor isn't all that difficult of a concept to grasp, even in our day.

Someone did write more extensively about Roman armor, filling in a few of the blanks for us. Roughly two hundred years before Paul penned his letter, the Greek historian Polybius left a detailed description of the various pieces worn by the Roman army. When he wrote about the breastplate, he said the foot soldiers had their own name for it. Paul used the term *thoraka* (that gives us the English word "thorax" or "torso"). However, the troops nicknamed the same piece of equipment as their *kardiopsulaka*, or "heart guard."

Calling the breastplate a heart guard brings its importance into sharp focus. It is there to protect the very center of our lives, both physically and emotionally. The heart not only sustains our bodies with every beat—it represents our will, our personality, our nature. No wonder the authors of the Bible warn us to never leave it exposed.

Proverbs 4:23
Above all else, guard your heart, for everything you do flows from it.

We instinctively agree with that wisdom. By nature, we're wired for self-preservation. But we don't normally reach for the breastplate of righteousness as the solution because we are busy cobbling together alternative heart guards.

We wall off our emotions, pushing them down to minimize the risk of being hurt. We build a persona, our "brand image" to keep people from seeing (and possibly rejecting) our true selves. And we keep ourselves distracted with the hopes that we can dull the ever-present ache of loneliness.

By and large, these homemade heart guards can do the trick, at least to a degree. But they come with a cost, because they don't just keep our hearts safe—they keep them from being known.

Nearly every Tuesday morning for well over a decade, I have met with my two friends, Scott and Tom. We started getting together with the simple idea that all of us wanted to have an authentic and transparent friendship, a little community where we could talk honestly about our real struggles and pray for each other.

Scott and Tom modeled openness, allowing me into their interior worlds. I welcomed their candor and sought to honor that trust. But whenever it was my turn to share about myself, I skated across the surface of my feelings, revealing little. I was doing pretty well, maybe a little tired. When it was time to ask for prayer, I could always fall back on the legitimate need for wisdom in preparing my next sermon. I could convey humility without having to divulge anything.

It wasn't a conscious decision to evade. Deflection came naturally, and my version of a heart guard did the work of keeping my inmost being out of sight.

Things continued that way for years. Then came my meltdown. Pain reached the point where I could no longer maintain that outward composure. As the walls crumbled and I finally let my friends in on the depth of my suffering for the first time, I experienced the unfamiliar sensation of allowing myself to be vulnerable.

To my amazement and relief, they didn't judge me. In fact, I discovered how significant it was for me to fall apart in front of these two men. I had no idea the amount of grace and compassion I had been missing. All my defenses had kept me from being truly known—and still loved.

There's no dark backside to the breastplate of righteousness.

Our attempts at self-protection have an element of hiding within them. Like Adam and Eve, we reach for the nearest, flimsy fig leaves, fearing exposure. We're convinced that what's inside our hearts is too raw and ugly to let anyone get close enough to see for themselves. And we grab on to anything that can insulate and isolate.

How can we protect our hearts in a healthier way, without cutting ourselves off from what we need most? Here is where Paul points us to a better defense. There's no dark backside to the breastplate of righteousness.

But it does raise questions, because we're not always clear in our minds about what righteousness even means. Our most common context for thinking about the term is *self*-righteousness, which immediately sours us to the word. Nobody likes encountering someone with the smug, judgmental air of sanctimony.

We generally equate the idea of a righteous person with someone who is expending themselves in pursuit of being good. Dictionary definitions of righteousness normally revolve around exemplary behavior and adhering to a strict set of values that can be justified as morally right.

When that's our understanding, we read the call to wear the breastplate of righteousness as a call to lead upright lives. We take the passage in Ephesians to mean our integrity will protect us, and our right behavior will be the thing to keep us safe.

Isn't that just a form of self-righteousness?

That's the opposite of what Paul hoped to communicate. He expressly states that in his letter to the church in Rome:

Romans 3:20
Therefore no one will be declared righteous in God's sight by the works of the law; rather, through the law we become conscious of our sin.

All those hoops I've been trying to jump through so carefully—they're not helping. I will never achieve a state of rightness through my efforts. In fact, the harder I work at following the rules, the more conscious I am of wanting to break them.

No matter how Christian it sounds, clean living makes no headway here. Praise God for a different route:

Romans 3:21-24
But now apart from the law the righteousness of God has been made known, to which the Law and the Prophets testify. This righteousness is given through faith in Jesus Christ to all who believe. There is no difference between Jew

and Gentile, for all have sinned and fall short of the glory
of God, and all are justified [righteousized] freely by his
grace through the redemption that came by Christ Jesus.

Hallelujah! A completely free gift, received by believing rather than behaving. All that is required is the trust that God is in fact offering this unearned righteousness to us.

Imagine a priceless vase that has been bumped from its pedestal and is in danger of crashing to the floor. Just in time, you reach out and catch it, tipping it back up and "setting it right." That is the righteousness of Christ—setting us back in our right relationship with God.

This is bread and butter gospel here. We're not breaking any new ground when we talk of this extraordinary reality. We count on the fact that the cross of Jesus welcomes us into his rightness. That is our one true heart guard.

I've known this and taught this for as long as I can remember. Yet it took a mental crisis to show me how little I live it. Despite all my professions to the contrary, I've continued to rely squarely on being right, all the while singing the praises of grace.

It is inherently and continually difficult to take in the true dimensions of what we've been given. P. T. Forsyth points to this:

It is a great thing to realize that the forgiving grace of
God is the deepest, mightiest, most permanent and
persistent power in the moral world . . . I beg you to
realize it, to arrest yourself, to compel yourself to stand
still long enough in the hurry of interests, the press of

pursuits, and the buzz of things, to take the fact and its meaning in.[19]

Inspired by his words, I conducted a very simple, personal exercise. First, I wrote down the negative words I regularly associate with myself, characteristics I felt were "un-right" about me. Words such as these came to mind easily:

CONFUSED	BROKEN	AFRAID
GUILTY	WOUNDED	FROZEN
ASHAMED	SMALL	WEAK

The list went on and on. Then, in an effort to "stare at grace" (as Forsyth suggested), I scratched them out one by one. I replaced each one with a new word, speaking to how God has covered me with his own righteousness, his "rightness."

~~CONFUSED~~ GUIDED	~~BROKEN~~ WHOLE	~~AFRAID~~ LOVED
~~GUILTY~~ FORGIVEN	~~WOUNDED~~ HEALED	~~FROZEN~~ FREED
~~ASHAMED~~ CONFIDENT	~~SMALL~~ PROTECTED	~~WEAK~~ STRENGTHENED

Not surprisingly, I was able to exchange every single negative word with one completely opposite. What's more, each of the new words found full support in Scripture. I didn't have to imagine something positive or put in what I wished for myself—they were all grounded in specific promises God has given.

Then something curious happened: a voice in my head began to dismiss the second list. As much as I knew these were solid, biblical truths, the harsh inner critic took over and presented me with all kinds of reasons why the new words didn't apply to me. Or why they were true, but with caveats. Or how this was a stupid, self-centered exercise to make myself feel better.

I am much more comfortable holding fast to the negative list and not turning, not "repenting" to consider the new list. It's far easier to stay fixated on all my perceived flaws, even when I know full well God sees me differently.

Why keep choosing the first list when I say I believe the second? Logically, I knew that if I was gravitating toward the negatives, they must be meeting a need. There had to be some benefit my mind thought it was getting. But what?

After further reflection, it became clear: focusing on the first list let me believe I was taking my brokenness seriously and doing something proactive about it. Keeping my faults at the front of mind felt like the responsible thing to do. Here was a way to salvage whatever scraps of righteousness I could find and still get some mileage out of them. It allowed me to say to God, "See? My goodness is offended by my badness. That has to count for something, doesn't it?"

The underlying assumption I had bought into was that *God looks on my self-judgment as admirable.* Never mind the fact that he says he has hurled my transgressions into the sea (Micah 7:19) or that he chooses to stop remembering my wrongdoings (Hebrews 8:12). Somehow, I have it in my head that he is pleased when I refuse to forgive and accept my own shortcomings.

In Roman armor, the design of the breastplate was much more form-fitting than the kind you see in classic medieval suits of armor. It was sculpted to the shape of a soldier's torso (albeit sometimes enhanced with a more chiseled six-pack than its owner).

In other words, the breastplate was cut in such a way that it wouldn't work to wear it over multiple layers of other armor; it had to be worn close to the body. Anyone outfitted with a heart guard would feel it pressing close, a constant reminder of both vulnerability and protection. It was the only thing between you and the blade of a sword or the tip of a spear.

> The underlying assumption I had bought into was that God looks on my self-judgment as admirable.

As we learn to count on Christ's righteousness, we become conscious of it being the only thing protecting us. I'd prefer to layer up, to "feel the burn" of zealous striving. I want the extra padding for good measure. But his heart guard must be worn up close and exclusively. That's the deal.

One of the primary strategies in OCD therapy is to intentionally put yourself in a context that triggers your anxiety, then resist the urge to respond the way that you normally would to make the feelings more manageable. Instead of adopting your favorite coping skills, you sit in the anxiety without trying to escape or alleviate it.

It's a difficult yet essential exercise in moving toward health. And it provides a fitting parallel to this idea of laying down our own heart guards. We resist the urge to try to keep ourselves safe. We stop attempting to be the ones orchestrating our own rescue.

It's one thing to put our trust in Christ at the start of our faith. It's another thing to live in that faith moment by moment, to count on nothing but God's love and compassion and mercy, to keep turning back to the second list of words. That's what keeps us in a place of humility and vulnerability. That's how we begin wearing the breastplate of righteousness.

I would like nothing more than to feel the truth of the second list as powerfully as I feel the weight of the first. I want that gut-level experience. I've prayed, "Lord, make your grace feel every bit as real as the shame and unworthiness I carry." I have read about heroes of the faith receiving a flash of revelation, and I covet something similar.

But that's not typically how faith works. God desires for us to live as if his words are true, regardless of the sensation we experience. He's asking for our confidence, not our pretending. Melody Beattie says, "We do not have to lie; we do not have to be dishonest with ourselves. We open up to the positive possibilities of the future, instead of limiting the future by today's feelings and circumstances."[20]

Though the fig tree may not blossom, we must trust the trustworthiness of his word and step into what we say we believe.

And as for where I direct all that desire to "do the right thing," I can go back to that second list for my reference point. What would it look like to act like a forgiven person? Would I be less petty and vindictive? If I see myself as fully loved and approved, how would it affect the way I compare myself to other people (and to my own rigid, impossible standards for myself)? What would it sound like to pray with full confidence? If shame and fear didn't hold sway in my decision making, how would my choices change?

Jesus said, "Blessed are those who hunger and thirst for righteousness, for they will be filled" (Matthew 5:6). He himself is our breastplate of righteousness, putting himself between us and peril, intercepting all attacks and repercussions. He alone puts everything right. And he calls us to ever-greater trust in that truth.

FOR REFLECTION

1. How would you explain righteousness to a child? What would you say to distinguish it from self-righteousness?

2. Make your own list of negative messages you hear in your head. Then counter each with a word from Christ. Which are hardest to believe?

3. Can you think of a practical step for transferring trust to Christ's righteousness in the way you live your life?

SEVEN

SHOD

*We never can thank God enough for giving
us not only a whole Gospel to believe,
but a whole world to give it to.*

A. B. Simpson

Back in ancient times, wealthy Romans had slaves who would follow them around, carrying their change of shoes. That way, after a day of walking the dusty roads, they could quickly slip on a clean pair of sandals before hosting guests or visiting one of the public baths. No one would ever be caught dead wearing their outdoor footwear inside. The appropriate shoes were always right at hand.

Scripture stands at our side, holding out the ideal shoes for us. The Apostle tells us to have our "feet fitted with the readiness that comes from the gospel of peace." The wording here is admittedly complex. But shoes go with readiness in nearly any culture in which they're worn. They are the last clothing item we don before heading out into the world. Parents herding the family toward the car will frequently say to their children, "Are you ready to go? Well, get your shoes on, then."

The spiritual shoes Paul recommends help us be prepared. The gospel of peace makes us ready. But ready for what? What exactly are we expected to do?

Paul's thinking about shoes was shaped by the stories he knew from Israel's past. One story in particular focused on the link between footwear and being prepared.

When God sent Moses to deliver the Israelites from slavery in Egypt, the clash with Pharaoh resulted in the ten plagues. The battle escalated until the last and terrible plague, wherein all the firstborn males in Egypt were struck down.

Each Israelite family escaped the same fate by taking a sacrificial lamb and putting some of its blood on their doorposts. The angel of death saw the blood and passed over them (foreshadowing the way the blood of Jesus, the Lamb of God, protects us).

The night that first Passover meal took place in Egypt, the Israelites were to partake of it in a very specific way.

Exodus 12:11
*This is how you are to eat it: with your cloak tucked into your belt, **your sandals on your feet** and your staff in your hand. Eat it in haste; it is the LORD's Passover.*

The entire community was to wear their shoes while they ate so they would be ready to leave as soon as they were done. They needed to get out of there in a hurry.

At this point, the miracle had happened. God had spared their lives.

But the purpose of the miracle was bigger than a reprieve from a death sentence. In his intervention, God created an opportunity for Israel to escape their enslavement. That's why he wanted them to get their feet in the game: *wearing gospel shoes makes us ready to move into freedom.*

Imagine if the Israelites had been so relieved when the angel of death passed over that they opted to stay in Egypt. With that kind of protection from God, why not just continue living there? The work was difficult, but if they could count on the Lord's support, things might not be so bad after all.

Yet remaining in slavery was never God's intention for his people. He acted on their behalf to liberate them from their oppression— not to simply make it more tolerable.

The pardon God has provided for us is staggering. His forgiveness deserves all our eternal gratitude and celebration. But there is a mobility implied in our rescue, because God has also given us shoes. His grace doesn't just cover the cost of our fallen state. It gives us the means to leave behind our age-old way of life. He calls us to step out from that which enslaves us and into genuine freedom.

In order to move, we first have to acknowledge that we're even living in the land of Egypt. Maybe you're thinking, "Nothing owns me."

The religious leaders said as much to Jesus (John 8:33). They didn't think they needed freedom. Jesus responded by telling them that to be a sinner is to be a slave, and to be a slave means you have no rights. When your owner calls, you must respond.

So much that is harmful can own us. We become attached to things that cannot meet our true desires, and we cannot break free. We crave what can never satisfy and pursue what we don't ultimately want. There is no end to the list of what can hold sway over us.

I positively hate it when my brain locks up and fixates on unwanted thoughts and feelings. It's torturous, and I expend a great deal of energy fighting it. Yet I often operate as if I owe my OCD something. It calls, and I respond as if duty-bound.

In a counseling session one day, my therapist held a notebook directly in front of my nose. "What can you see?" he asked. The question had such an obvious answer it was hardly worth asking. I couldn't see anything but paper.

"This is what your mind is doing," he continued, still holding the yellow legal pad. "It is making it so you can't pay attention to anything or anyone else around you. What is that doing for you?"

I couldn't answer that one. I had to go home and sit with it until the following session before I understood. And then I saw it: the problem was the solution. My OCD was taking me out of the room. It preoccupied me to the point where I no longer had to deal with whatever was right in front of me.

Even though the OCD was negative and causing me pain, in a most unhealthy way, it still provided a form of escape that gave relief from real-world anxieties. As long as my mind stayed busy with imagined threats, I didn't have to grapple with the present. And my brain had me convinced there would be dire consequences if I didn't keep obsessing over the non-existent concerns. It kept me in a tight bind.

When we want to do good, evil is right there with us. Whatever holds us captive, we cannot emancipate ourselves: we require grace. Praise God, we have it in Jesus. And he has given us the shoes to move out.

Our journey into greater freedom is lifelong. But we can depend on God to be enough. He will supply the manna and the pillar of fire. Everything we need will be provided along the way.

We find this to be true even in the rugged nature of the shoes Paul describes, because they don't simply prepare us to move—*gospel shoes make us ready for a long walk.*

As part of their training, Roman soldiers participated in what they called a "loaded" march. Carrying a forty-five-pound rucksack, they trekked roughly eighteen miles within six hours. Then they had to repeat the exercise, but in the second round, they were required to go twenty-four miles in the same amount of time. Soldiers did not advance to weapons training until they had mastered the fundamentals of marching.

In its heyday, the vast Roman empire covered nearly 1.7 million square miles. That's a lot of ground to cover on foot. Legions of troops spent a far larger percentage of their time marching than in combat. And good shoes were essential for the monotonous task of walking and walking and walking.

Marching is often our biggest battle: that daily plodding forward, the repetitive motion of following in the footsteps of Christ. Our need for grace is easily recognized during major crises that come our way. We are quick to cry out when we're desperate. But the shoes of the gospel are walking shoes, intended for everyday wear. God's grace equally covers the boredom and monotony and hard plodding of ordinary life.

I am not a "process" person. I much prefer closure and completion. This ties back to my anxiety around being good enough. In my brain, *unfinished* equals *unacceptable* and outside of God's will. If God wants me to arrive at the destination of being mature and holy, so my thinking goes, anything short of that feels wrong and inadequate. My options are then limited to either perfection or failure. Getting where I'm going becomes urgent, and I need to run—not march—to the finish line.

> Being a work under construction isn't a concession, it is part of a divine design.

The incarnation of Christ settles me back down. God put his stamp of approval on process when he sent his Son into the world as a baby. The angels may have declared "Peace on earth" to the shepherds, but there were still three decades to go before the fulfillment of that peace on the cross. It was not instantly achieved or implemented. The majority of Jesus' life on earth was spent maturing into an adult, "[growing] in wisdom and stature" (Luke 2:52). He came to bring salvation, but he had to slog through adolescence first.

That should tell us something. If experiencing all the developmental stages of life didn't taint Christ's holiness—if a slow unfolding was part of God's pre-ordained plan for him—that means God doesn't expect me to rush my way through growth. Being a work under construction isn't a concession; it is part of a divine design.

Marching is walking at a set pace, not speeding up to arrive faster. The deliberate rhythm of walking causes us to trust the arrival will happen in its own time.

Most days we do not wake up in the morning and find we are significantly more Christlike than the day before. Today's struggles don't look very different from yesterday's. We have more times of trudging along than moments of miraculous transformation, and change feels excruciatingly slow.

In his book, *Three Mile an Hour God*, Kosuke Koyama says, "God walks 'slowly' because he is love. If he is not love he would have gone much faster. . . . It is the speed we walk and therefore it is the speed the love of God walks."[21]

In the end, we discover that God's patience becomes the birthplace for ours. He allows us time and opportunity for incremental, sometimes glacial-paced, growth. He knows how much (or little) we bruised reeds can handle at any one time.

Sometimes, God's will for us doesn't involve any moving at all, but rather staying in place. *The gospel shoes make us ready to stand our ground.*

Roman soldiers wore a type of shoes called *caliga*, and they were more of a boot than a sandal. This provided extra support to keep ankles from turning in a fight. Caliga also had hard leather soles with knobby metal nails like cleats on the bottom. The nails gave them outstanding grip. They could lodge themselves in the ground and keep a soldier in place when an enemy was pressing close.

I live in the Pacific Northwest, where Mt. Rainier proves an irresistible draw for hikers. One friend of mine who summited the mountain found the experience brought him face to face with his deepest fears. Making it to the top meant traversing treacherous sections of the trail that were nearly vertical sheets of ice.

His boots were fitted with crampons, the metal traction spikes made for crossing frozen terrain. There were times he had to trust himself completely to the integrity of those crampons, because they were all that was keeping him from plummeting over the side of a drop-off.

The gospel secures us. We don't even see how perilously close to the edge we are at times, with countless forces that would sweep us off the cliff. That's why nearly all of Paul's letters include the admonition to "stand firm."

But on what? Many Christians today feel the rug has been pulled out from under them. They are deconstructing the faith of their upbringing, reexamining long-held beliefs that could not provide solid footing in the rapidly changing world. They see the cracks in the foundation of all they were once taught and are unwilling to simply pretend it makes sense anymore.

This should not come as a surprise. If my earlier premise is true that much of what we bill as Christian isn't about faith, then the ground was destined to crumble eventually. When the gospel has been displaced, it's no wonder people abandon Christianity in disillusionment.

Yet often the response of church leaders has been simply to decry the exodus from their pews without giving more than cursory attention to the validity of the dissatisfaction and the underlying concerns. It calls to mind the words of the prophet: "They dress the wound of my people as though it were not serious" (Jeremiah 6:14).

Questioning tradition is healthy, and jettisoning old baggage is essential for revitalizing and reforming faith. Jesus himself turned over tables both literally and figuratively. The current wave of dissatisfaction with status quo Christianity in America ought to be heeded and honored, because it is leading to much-needed pruning of the church. As Russell Moore put it, "Let's not mistake hurt for rebellion, trauma for infidelity, or a broken heart for an empty soul."[22]

Of course, there are downsides to endless deconstruction. Disbelief adopted as a permanent posture cannot ultimately land anywhere, because it does not allow us to accept anything without jeopardizing our stance. Inquiry becomes simply an exercise in proving everything can be dismantled rather than an honest search for what is true and real.

But to continue with our shoe analogy, sometimes rocks get lodged inside and need to be shaken out. We have Scripture's full blessing to cast off every bit of religious nonsense that trips us up and gets in the way (Hebrews 12:1). The gospel suffers no harm under scrutiny and offers room for the tightly bound soul to explore.

The more we experience that personally, the more we will want other people to know it, too. That's because *the gospel shoes make us ready to run with hope.*

Paul's words to the Ephesians make me think of the passage from Isaiah:

Isaiah 52:7

How beautiful on the mountains
are the feet of those who bring good news,
who proclaim peace,
who bring good tidings,
who proclaim salvation,
who says to Zion, "Your God reigns!"

You can picture a messenger, dispatched from the front lines where an important battle has been fought. He runs to share the outcome with the people back home. Everyone in town anxiously awaits the report, when suddenly the runner bursts up over the hill shouting, "We won! We won! The war is over!"

Being the one to bring that message of relief and joy is hardly a burden. It's a high privilege. So why does sharing the good news about Jesus often feel like such a guilt-inducing chore?

For much of my life, evangelism as a concept has put me in a bind. I have worn the weight of Christian duty heavily and have felt burdened to witness to people, not so much out of concern for them as out of compulsion to do the right thing. At the same time, the awkwardness of imposing my views on someone else has made me hesitate for fear of offending.

The way out of the dilemma has been to evangelize myself. By that I mean this: a fresh, personal encounter with the good news has offered me a different way in.

If we return to our messenger for a moment, he could shout the news boldly because he had seen the victory himself. It was a firsthand account. There is much more freedom and confidence when you know of what you speak.

As I have experienced the gospel's power in the midst of my battle with anxiety, it has given me far more freedom in sharing my faith. It's become a firsthand report of the good news I've known personally. I'm no longer trying to convince someone or win an argument about doctrine or explain salvation perfectly. I'm simply telling my own story of grace. It's easier to talk about your favorite shoes when they've really become your favorite.

Still, we're not always convinced anyone wants to hear the good news. It's one thing to discuss finding peace with God in a church context, but the average person on the street is not consciously worrying about their sinfulness and any barrier it might create between them and God. That is a largely foreign concept that doesn't tap into a felt need. With no concern over estrangement, the gospel of peace lands on deaf ears.

> It is easier to talk about your favorite shoes when they've really become your favorite.

That being said, you don't have to look far to see that peace (or the lack of it) in broad terms does seem to be very much on everyone's minds. A worldwide pandemic has a way of revealing and cultivating unrest and division in all spheres of life. Everyone can now identify with the widespread desire for hope and change.

Consider the following:

UNPEACEFUL STATISTICS

- 77% of Americans experience physical symptoms of stress.
- 73% experience psychological symptoms.
- Depression is the leading cause of disability worldwide.
- 40 million American adults suffer from an anxiety disorder.
- 80 million American adults have high blood pressure.
- One in three deaths are caused by heart attack and stroke.

Sources: The Anxiety & Depression Association of America (www.adaa.org)
The American Institute of Stress (www.stress.org)

People are quite literally dying for some peace. They would love to hear good news that results in less stress. And it is no stretch of the gospel to show how peace *with God and peace from God go hand in hand.*

Philippians 4:7
And the peace of God, which transcends all understanding, will guard your hearts and your minds in Christ Jesus.

1 Peter 5:7
Cast all your anxiety on him because he cares for you.

Struggle has deepened my personal connection to the gospel of peace. It has stuffed my feet further into the shoes than ever and made it easier for me to want to share my hope.

Why? Not because I'm so worry-free now, but because my soul has crossed a desert and found water. My testimony has been expanded and added to the chorus of millions who have learned for themselves that God is full of rescue, that he is with us forever, and that we can transfer the load to him that is too much to bear.

The gospel is still what we need. It's the shoe that always fits. And Jesus is the ground that will always hold.

FOR REFLECTION

1. Do any examples come to mind of how God has walked at your pace with you? Why do you think the gospel's effect in our lives moves so slowly?

2. Can you identify any aspects of your faith that you are deconstructing right now? How does that feel?

3. Where in your story has the gospel felt most active and alive? Where do you wish it would? Take a moment to talk to God about that.

EIGHT

SHIELDS UP

Much-Afraid stood quite still,
looking up into his face,
which now had such a happy,
exultant look, the look of
one who above all else delights
in saving and delivering.

Hannah Hurnard, *Hinds' Feet on High Places*

A miracle turtle named Freddy (who happens to be a female) survived a forest fire in Brazil. In the blaze, she lost eighty-five percent of her shell. A tortoise can't live long in that condition. Exposed and traumatized, the poor creature caught pneumonia twice and wouldn't eat for a month.

Then a group from Sao Paulo calling themselves "The Animal Avengers" swooped in to rescue Freddy and nurse her back to health. The effort took three veterinarians, a surgeon, and a graphic designer to create a prosthetic replacement shell for her. Precision engineering went into every aspect of the design. They even researched turtle markings and meticulously painted the shell so it could pass for a natural one.

It's a lovely story of great kindness. All that time, expense, energy, and care to protect one small animal. From a financial standpoint, it defies logic for such a large crew to invest so heavily in the future of a single tortoise. And yet, as Freddy's recovery can attest, the result is beautiful and life-giving.

The shield of faith is one of God's many exorbitant gifts to us, a shell of protection as mystifying as it is vital. John's first letter tells us God has "lavished" his love on us (1 John 3:1), and this piece of the armor reflects that extravagant care.

As we have seen, Paul provides rather slim details on most components of our spiritual armor. But when he speaks of the shield of faith, he gives us a bit more insight as to its value:

Ephesians 6:16

In addition to all this, take up the shield of faith, with which you can extinguish all the flaming arrows of the evil one.

Manufacturers in the security industry have developed a composite metal foam to be used in bullet-proof vests. It not only blocks a round of ammunition from hitting the wearer—it completely pulverizes the bullet. Video footage from product testing shows armor-piercing bullets disintegrating upon contact with the foam. The impenetrable surface leaves bullets with nowhere to go.

According to Ephesians, the shield of faith goes beyond resisting the devil's fiery darts because it reduces them to ashes. They disintegrate on contact. The word Paul chose for shield describes the larger, rectangular type favored by the Romans (as opposed to the small, circular kind). An army could line them up, side by side, to create a formidable wall. When projectiles flew through the air, the legionaries would hunker down in a cluster and hold the shields above their heads to create a dome of safety.

While such images capture the indispensable nature of the shield (not to mention the power of fellowship), I must confess it has been difficult for me to translate the concept into my own life. My therapist once told me matter-of-factly that people who suffer from OCD are characterized by low levels of trust. I didn't much care to hear that, but his words had the ring of truth.

Faith is not my first reflex. In fact, I'd rather not exercise it. I go out of my way to reduce the reasons why I might need to leave a situation in God's care. I deliberately structure my life to minimize uncertainty. My fears of doing the wrong thing, thinking the wrong thing, feeling the wrong thing—they all gang up to prevent me from boldly trusting God.

> It is strangely easy to profess a belief in God without relying on his support.

Consequently, the shield of faith has been one of the most challenging pieces of the armor for me to pick up. Intellectually, I want to consider myself a person who lives by faith, but when my anxieties kick in, I retreat to my own self-protection instead.

It is strangely easy to profess a belief in God without relying on his support. The conversations we avoid, the dreams we don't pursue, the money we can't give away, the conflicts we postpone—they can all be strategies to eliminate our need to count on him. How do we raise the shield of faith?

In a transparent account of her own story, author Juanita Ryan beautifully describes how she leaned into faith through a season where trusting God seemed impossible.

When our son was addicted to drugs, lying about his use and growing more and more paranoid, the phrase, "Trust God" took on an entirely new and desperate meaning for me. It sounded like I was being told, "Let go of your son even though it feels like he will fall to his death. Let go of him and trust that God will catch and hold him and care for him." This seemed impossible to me. I felt like I was being asked to do the impossible.

But it is what I had to do. I could no longer put my trust in my abilities to fix the problem. Only God could restore our son. My work was to entrust myself and our son and our entire family to God's loving care. Every day. Multiple times a day. Trusting God was no longer a simple slogan. It took on urgent meaning. It became something visceral. At first it was like performing a high-wire act, expecting to fall at any moment, but choosing to believe that there was a safety net beneath us even though I could not see the net or understand how it could catch us . . .

A friend who was praying for us told me in the midst of our darkest days that she sensed that God was inviting me to rest. Rest! The word startled me. It seemed so bizarre in my circumstances. And yet I could feel the difference it would make. I could climb down from my imaginary high-wire act and crawl into God's loving arms. And rest. For me this became the deepest, truest meaning of the word trust.[23]

Can I do that? Can I grow my confidence in God and rest from my own attempts to control the situation? Faith means relinquishing my hold on so many things:

THE PROBLEM I CAN'T SOLVE

THE QUESTION I CAN'T ANSWER

THE WRONG I CAN'T RIGHT

THE PERSON I CAN'T CHANGE

THE FUTURE I CAN'T SEE

THE SIN I CAN'T FORGIVE

THE SITUATION I CAN'T ALTER

GOD'S CARE

How does entrusting God with all these aspects of our lives function as a shield? When I was growing up, the connection seemed straightforward: if you believed in God, you were spared pain. When there seemed to be an exception to that rule, I suspected it was most likely due to faulty faith on the part of the person suffering.

My entire family was steeped in Christianity. Not only my immediate family, but also cousins, aunts, uncles, and grandparents on both sides professed a faith in God. Until I reached high school, I was exposed to very few tragedies among any of my relatives, and I would have attributed this sheltered state to the shield of faith guarding our household. Bad things happened to other people, but not to us. I presumed it was the natural result of our faith.

That outlook only lasts as long as the skies stay clear and the delusion remains unchallenged. Eventually, life catches up. It proved a shock to my belief system when I saw members of my own family experience great trauma. Inexplicably, hardship showed up in my own back yard. Loss and pain entered the bubble. The shield, to my way of thinking, malfunctioned.

As I grew older and my paradigm shifted to account for these realities, I assumed faith would at the very least minimize the depth of suffering and give it meaning. God might allow tough times to enter my life once in a while, but the duration would be shorter, the intensity would be lessened, and his purposes would be clear.

This, too, proved a misguided concept of the shield of faith.

In Hebrews 11, the word faith appears twenty-seven times—a more concentrated exploration of faith than anywhere else in the Bible. The chapter provides example after example of women and men who courageously bet everything on God as they endured an extraordinary array of circumstances:

Hebrews 11:36-39

Some faced jeers and flogging, and even chains and imprisonment. They were put to death by stoning; they were sawed in two; they were killed by the sword. They went about in sheepskins and goatskins, destitute, persecuted and mistreated—the world was not worthy of them. They wandered in deserts and mountains, living in caves and in holes in the ground. These were all commended for their faith, yet none of them received what had been promised . . .

Here we have those the Bible elevates as examples of individuals entrusting themselves to God. You would be hard pressed to find greater models for raising the shield of faith. And what does the text say? Some ended up having their bodies cut in half! Others were forced to live in holes in the ground. None of them saw God's promises play out in the way their lives unfolded.

Bad circumstances don't cancel God's promises.

Even Paul, as he wrote down his thoughts about the armor of God, did so while sitting chained up as a prisoner, suffering greatly. That being the case, his contention that faith is a shield must mean something drastically different than I have imagined it. It must not mean faith will spare me from hardship. It must not mean God will automatically bless me, make me healthy, or remove obstacles from my path every time I pray.

And it must not mean the lack of blessing indicates something is wrong or faith doesn't work. Bad circumstances don't cancel God's promises.

Wherever I got the idea that a life of trust would result in fewer problems, it didn't come from Scripture. This is a relief to realize, because it means I no longer have to try and reconcile the discrepancy between what I thought faith was supposed to do for me and the lack of change I see in my situation.

What are we to make of the shield, then? Part of the answer lies in what Paul said about the armor of God in its entirety:

> For our struggle is not against flesh and blood, but against the rulers, against the authorities, against the powers of this dark world and against the spiritual forces of evil in the heavenly realms.

Paul recognized that if our enemies in question are not other humans, the battle isn't primarily raging in the material world. The shield of faith isn't so much a barrier to physical harm or relational conflict as it is a means to preserve us in the midst of spiritual dangers. The fiery darts are aimed at our very souls.

Jesus refers to Satan as "a liar and the father of lies" (John 8:44). Deception is his weapon of choice. If we trace his interactions with humanity all the way back to the Garden of Eden, we can see he hasn't changed tactics very much over time. His goal is to disrupt our relationship with God, to sow all the seeds of doubt and distrust that he can.

Again and again, he routinely reaches for some variation of the same two pernicious little firebrands, niggling lies that wedge their way in to undermine our capacity to receive God's love:

TWO FIERY ARROWS

1 I'm not good enough for God.

2 God's not good enough for me.

The first category of arrows includes all the accusations we hear in our heads that leave us questioning ourselves. The voices are convincing and have a familiar ring:

If anyone knew the real you, they'd reject you.

You're so lazy.

You'll never be like _____.

You're exactly like _____.

No one could ever love you.

You don't belong here.

If that was your best...

You're too broken to help.

You ruin everything.

(Fill in the blank) _____.

These cruel indictments often sound to our ears as if they are God's own pronouncements about us. They have a note of correction in them that would have us believe they carry divine authority.

But these crushing messages differ greatly from the Holy Spirit's conviction of sin in our lives. Where conviction leads toward change and restoration, accusation demoralizes and induces shame. Shame would have us believe that not only are our actions wrong—our very selves are unacceptable.

The devil's lie—that we're inherently beyond remedy—can only lead us in one of two directions. We either hide to prevent anyone from seeing how bad we are, or we white-knuckle it and strain to transform ourselves into something different. Both options require an exhausting amount of energy to maintain. And they prevent us from experiencing the love already there for us.

The second kind of fiery arrow Satan hurls our direction seeks to throw into question the character of God himself, to suggest he is unkind, untrustworthy, or untruthful. The devil would have us second-guess everything our Father has said about himself and all he has ever done for us.

So, in the serpent's crafty reinterpretation, God's prohibition to Adam and Eve regarding the fruit becomes a mark of his stinginess rather than evidence of his caring protection (Serpent: "The fruit is actually good for you!"). His warnings of the consequences are exaggerated (Serpent: "You won't really die."). And his motive for doing so looks suspect (Serpent: "He just doesn't want you to become like him.").

For us, the messages have a similar tone, leaving us skeptical that God has our best interest at heart:

A good God wouldn't let me feel this way.

If I trust God with _____, he will let me down.

God's motivations are suspect.

_____ will prove more fulfilling than God for me.

If God really cared, he would show it by _____

My sense of morality/justice/judgment/timing beats God's.

God doesn't care about my happiness.

The enemy loves to stir up this kind of dissatisfaction within us, convincing us that there is something else out there promising a better hope. The world is full of ready substitutes for God, miniature idols we clutch, not realizing, as Isaiah said, that the thing in our hand is a lie (Isaiah 44:20). As Simone Weil wrote, "At the centre of the human heart, is the longing for an absolute good, a longing which is always there and is never appeased by any object in this world."[24]

God's response for fending off both types of arrows can be best seen in the cross of Christ. By his death, Jesus stepped in front of us, placing himself as a shield between us and our enemy, taking the full brunt of Satan's attacks.

Psalm 91:3 reminds readers of this hope: "Surely he will save you from the fowler's snare and from the deadly pestilence." The next verse indicates how God brings about our deliverance: "He will cover you with his feathers, and under his wings you will find refuge."

In the psalm writer's analogy, we are all birds, caught in the trap of a hunter. Unable to release ourselves, we cry out for help. But the answer is surprising: God also has feathers and wings. To set us free, God became a bird himself and climbed down inside the trap next to us, offering his own wings as a refuge.

That's the gospel. Jesus is our shield of faith because he has climbed down inside the human condition with us, turning himself into our shelter from harm.

All the lies trying to burn themselves into our brains, all the vicious voices, are met by the fiercely protective love of Christ. When we raise him as our defense, the fiery darts have nowhere to land. There's no need to justify ourselves to our accuser or prove why we're okay—we are fully accepted by God. Our own goodness isn't even up for discussion because we're standing behind the goodness of Christ. That's what's shielding us. No matter how incessantly the arrows may hurtle toward us, God's love for us is unassailable.

And it is in that love, displayed most fully on the cross, where God gives us everything that can satisfy our deepest needs and desires. Earlier in Ephesians, Paul wrote,

Ephesians 1:3
Praise be to the God and Father of our Lord Jesus Christ, who has blessed us in the heavenly realms with every spiritual blessing in Christ.

A past-perfect statement. God *has* blessed us, and that accomplishment cannot be undone. Every conceivable good for our souls and spirits has been handed to us in Christ.

I return to the scene I described at the beginning of the book, where I was lying awake, desperately reaching for the shield of faith and finding nothing but disappointment. I expected faith to prevent the arrows from flying that night, and I couldn't understand why they kept coming.

The job of a shield is to deflect attacks, not end them. I am beginning to learn they don't have to stop for me to be okay. Distressing as they might be, they ultimately have no power to damage my standing in Christ.

What does it sound like to claim that, to raise Jesus as your shield? Can you talk back to your anxiety and say, "This is to be expected. I can do hard things with Jesus. I can catch my breath and step back from the situation, allowing the waves of fear to wash over me. I will still be standing with Christ at my side after they have come and gone"?

> The job of a shield is to deflect attacks, not end them.

Like a fierce rainstorm pelting a tin roof, the noise outside may be deafening, but it poses no threat to those inside. Even when the arrows grow louder as they hiss their way toward me, Christ intercepts them all and extinguishes their flames. I am safe forever in the shelter of his wings.

FOR REFLECTION

1. How has the shield of faith looked different than you expected?

2. Revisit the list of concerns placed in God's care. Which are most challenging for you to entrust to him?

3. If the devil has two types of fiery arrows ("You're not good enough for God," "God's not good enough for you"), which of the two comes your way most?

NINE

PRAYING FOR MY BASAL GANGLIA

Is he mad? Anyway there's something on his mind, as sure as there must be something on a deck when it cracks.

Herman Melville, *Moby Dick*

The mind suffers and the body cries out.

Cardinal Lamberto,
Mario Puzo's *The Godfather III*

While swimming in the ocean, an Australian photographer happened upon an unexpected sight: a small, golden-colored fish swam past, its head completely encased in the translucent body of a jellyfish. Still alive, the fish seemed to be steering the jellyfish where it wanted to go.

The photographer wasn't sure what to do. Had the little fish unwittingly become trapped to the point where it needed rescue? Was the jellyfish in the middle of eating the fish for dinner?

It turned out neither was the case. The fish was a trevally, a species known to wrap themselves in jellyfish as if strapping on a see-through helmet. It's a defensive maneuver to avoid becoming part of the food chain. Larger predators are so afraid of getting stung by jellyfish that they will leave the trevally alone and search elsewhere for a meal.

I'm grateful for all of God's armor, but my season of mental duress has given me a special affection for the helmet of salvation. If I could, I would climb completely inside it like that little fish, wrapping myself with the kind of protection my enemies will fear.

We most often associate the word *salvation* with our eternal destiny. To our way of thinking, salvation equals going to heaven. But its reach is so much bigger. The cross was not simply about a future transaction, saving our souls from damnation someday. The work it accomplished reverberates through every moment of our daily existence. Salvation is happening here and now.

Things do not always appear that way. Life continues to be full of pain and suffering that would make us question the effectiveness of the helmet we've been given. We have difficulty seeing how Christ is preserving in the moment.

When my oldest son was in middle school, I took him up to the mountains for snowboarding lessons. Neither one of us had ever tried it before, and I am not exactly (or even inexactly) athletic.

After a few successful runs on the bunny hill, I was feeling confident I could attempt the actual slope. Looking down from the chair lift,

I could see it was a much steeper hill than the gentle incline where we had been practicing.

Unsteady and unsure, I worked my way down the mountain by inching the board forward sideways, never quite mastering the proper snowboard technique. Yet in true, stereotypical-male fashion, I determined to hang in there as long as my son did (who, by the way, was already far down the slope.)

This continued for a few more laborious cycles. Finally, it came time for the last run of the day. I should have listened to my twitching leg muscles and called it quits before ever returning to the top. But, clinging to some false idea that I was improving, I chose to give it one more shot.

Picking up speed, I forgot everything I was supposed to do. I lost my balance and fell hard, smacking my head with enough force to make me see stars, hurtling end over end with the board until I came to rest on my back. I had a headache for a solid month. The only thing that saved me from far more serious injury was the fact that I had been wearing an industrial strength helmet when I crashed.

Here's what I can tell you: the helmet didn't improve my snowboarding skills. It didn't turn me into an athlete. And it wasn't able to prevent the fall from happening. But it did exactly what it was supposed to do, which was preserve my life.

Sometimes we may think the helmet of salvation isn't working for us. We still fall. We still feel like we are under attack, and we wonder how God is allowing everything to happen. But as we said in the last chapter, the armor isn't there to prevent the arrows or bullets from flying. It's not even designed to prevent us from getting knocked to the ground. It's there to preserve our life. And it silently safeguards us through our day-to-day struggles.

This is what allowed Paul to say, "We are hard pressed on every side, but not crushed" (2 Corinthians 4:8a). It's what gave Peter confidence that we can rejoice even when we have had to "suffer grief in all kinds of trials" (1 Peter 1:6). It is how James could celebrate distress, how John understood Christ is greater than the world, how Jude knew God could keep us from falling.

The devil continues to assault Christ's followers daily with accusations and doubt. We sin, we grow weary, we question our faith and our faithfulness. Our sense of well-being and commitment fluctuates moment by moment. Yet through it all, Jesus says, "No one will snatch them out of my hand" (John 10:28). The helmet of salvation is continually in place.

It certainly didn't seem like it when my interior world began to crumble. I kept saying, "It feels like my brain is broken." My mind had been my sanctum sanctorum, my sacred retreat from the pressures of life. And now somehow the enemy had breached my highest walls and reached me in my most well-defended stronghold.

It was so disorienting. My brain was short-circuiting. My head was no longer safe, and I grieved the loss of that refuge. As the pain continued to grow, the helmet of salvation moved from word picture to lifesaving necessity.

It was while struggling to make sense of my meltdown that I learned I was exhibiting all the symptoms of scrupulosity. Within the broader scope of OCD, scrupulosity is a disorder of the conscience: the spiritual equivalent of compulsive hand-washing wherein you can never scrub yourself clean.

Up until this point, I had always considered my hypersensitive conscience to be a rather admirable trait. My halo shone just a little bit brighter than everyone else's because I cared so much about sin. I was a suffering saint, burdened with a desire for holiness that was out of reach for the masses. I wouldn't have phrased it that way, but I prided myself on my above-and-beyond concern over right and wrong.

> What I thought was me at my best was in reality a place where I deeply needed grace.

And now here I was, suddenly learning what I thought had been a strength was actually a distress signal. My badge of honor turned out to show indications of mental disorder and dysfunction. *What I thought was me at my best was in reality a place where I deeply needed grace.*

That revelation proved more than humbling; it changed my self-perception. My identity had been linked tightly to my self-control. I lived for doing the right thing, gaining my sense of well-being from performing up to expectations. Suddenly I found myself in a place where I was out of control, where my mind was defying my will. I was powerless to stop it. Try as I might, I finally had to admit, "I can't." And in response, Christ said, "I know."

My newfound helplessness led me to a far more personal understanding of the grace I had always preached. I found myself clinging to it like never before, gulping it down because my thirsty soul couldn't get enough.

I also gained a deeper compassion for people experiencing all types of mental anguish. In the past, I tended to view anyone struggling with anxiety as needing to come in line with the myriad of Scripture passages that tell us not to be anxious, worried, or afraid. Viewed through my singular filter of right and wrong, it was a simple matter of choosing to obey what the Bible said and give up fear.

I read those verses very differently now. Thankfully, they sound full of reassurance rather than full of reprimand. The Lord who will not break a bruised reed does not punish his children for being in crisis.

Psalm 94:19 says, "When anxiety was great within me, your consolation brought me joy." Consolation, not chastisement, is the salve. When someone is experiencing suffering that is both irrational and involuntary, we must take great care to not multiply their pain by mischaracterizing it as sinful.

> The Lord who will not break a bruised reed does not punish his children for being in crisis.

Anxiety is highly complex, an intermingling of cognitive, emotional, and spiritual elements. The body factors in as well. According to psychiatrist Dr. Ian Osborn, "OCD has been officially recognized as being just as 'biologically based' as diabetes or heart disease ..."[25]

Scientists have found a distinct physical component that plays a role in OCD: a cluster of neurons near the base of the brain called the basal ganglia. Buried deep in the center of the brain, the basal ganglia tells your body which circumstances pose a threat requiring a response. Dr. Joel Frohlich describes it this way: "Like a secret agent, we only notice the basal ganglia when it does its job wrong. This secret agent of the brain facilitates wanted behaviors and stops unwanted behaviors."[26]

If the basal ganglia becomes damaged in some way (caused by anything from a virus to a lack of oxygen), thoughts that would normally be ignored as just unpleasant or unwanted are mistakenly interpreted as dangerous.

Dr. Eric Klinger has shown through his research that the average person thinks approximately four thousand distinct thoughts each day. Of those, roughly five hundred will be unwanted, "intrusive" ideas. A normally functioning basal ganglia will dismiss the extraneous thoughts, allowing them to slip downstream and out of consciousness. But when that part of the brain malfunctions, the unimportant thoughts snag and register as harmful, causing fear and requiring inordinate attention. What should be dismissible cannot be dismissed.[27]

I found it strangely comforting to hear I have a misfiring basal ganglia. Not that I needed a scapegoat to blame for what I was experiencing, but it gave me a name. Now I had something specific I could pray about. My basal ganglia became symbolic of my anxiety.

Initially, armed with this new information, I prayed for God to fix my basal ganglia. "Whatever is wrong with it, heal it up and make it better." My heart was quick to assume that would be God's primary desire for me, too. After all, isn't he the Great Physician?

I had this distinct visual of a poisoned thorn lodged in my head. That's what it felt like, and I just wanted someone to remove it. Yet as soon as that image came to mind, it inevitably took me to Paul, praying unsuccessfully for the extraction of his own thorn. And I realized God might have other things he could do with this trial than simply end it.

When you can name something and put words around it, you take away its power. Speaking the name of my basal ganglia out loud is my defiant act to diminish its authority over me.

The Bible says the name of Jesus is above every name. I have come to believe that does not just include personal names and titles. *Every named thing must come under the authority of the name above all names.* By naming my basal ganglia, I could say, "Jesus, your name is bigger than this. This is under your care."

JESUS

basal ganglia

No matter what caused my anxiety, no matter what part of the blame I bear for my own mess, no matter what role the devil plays in attacking my mind, if I am offering it up to Jesus, God wins, and the devil loses.

Victory, it turns out, is much bigger than freedom from anxiety. It is freedom from the power of anxiety. I do not need it to disappear—God is inviting me to trust him in the face of it. Instead of treating it like a threat inside my head, I can think of it the way I would tinnitus. The ringing in my ears may remain, but it is only background noise. If I lean in and concentrate past it, I can still enjoy the music of life that is much richer and more important.

Praise God he is answering the bigger prayer for me. While I still wouldn't choose to repeat the mental anguish, I can honestly say I am grateful for what has come out of this struggle. And when I sense the familiar dread and uncertainty creeping into my consciousness, it does not own me the way it once did. Even a basal ganglia must bow to the name of Jesus.

My therapist gave me an exercise in which I visualize myself on the battlefield with all my fearful thoughts racing toward me. Then, rather than engaging them, I simply stand firm as Paul instructed, and wait for the Lord to fight for me.

I think about the helmet of salvation in new terms now. Have you ever seen someone in the hospital who has experienced major head trauma or undergone a brain operation? Often, doctors will have a patient wear a helmet to protect the damaged skull and hold it in place.

The helmet of salvation isn't only for preventing injuries from the outside. It also protects our already wounded heads. Whatever horrors rage inside our minds are covered by the blood of Jesus.

When I think of the crown of thorns digging into Christ's head, I see all the poisonous barbs from my own mind transferred to him. And that renews my mind.

Jesus said he is the Way, and I imagine him being the way in my brain, mapping new paths for my mind to travel, new synapses for the neurons. And all the while, I am cradled by the helmet of salvation, guarding me from what is outside, and keeping what is inside safe under his care.

> The helmet of salvation isn't only for preventing injuries from the outside. It also protects our already wounded heads.

I also envision pith helmets, the kind worn with khaki shorts and cargo vests in old jungle safari movies. Those odd-looking hats were literally made from pith, or cork. Explorers would soak them in water overnight, then place the saturated helmets on their heads. As the water in the helmets evaporated, it would keep them cool under the hot African sun.

Wearing the helmet of salvation can be as simple as soaking in the truth of Jesus. Saturating ourselves with thoughts of him cools the fire in our heads.

What is occupying a disproportionate place in your thoughts? What has you worried or sidetracked? Name it. Call it out and say, "I am placing you where you belong: beneath the authority of Christ himself."

It may not go away. But it cannot have first place. There is only one name written across the top of all the world. Everything else must take the knee.

FOR REFLECTION

1. Have you ever had a realization that changed your perception of yourself?

2. What do you think of the idea that we don't need to be free of our problems so much as we need to be free from their power in our minds? What's the difference?

3. What "named thing" can you place under the name of Jesus?

TEN

THE SECRET TO SWORD FIGHTING

You Christians look after a document
containing enough dynamite to blow all
civilization to pieces, turn the world upside
down and bring peace to a battle-torn
planet. But you treat it as though it is nothing
more than a piece of literature.

Mahatma Gandhi

Galgano Guidotti was a bit of a wild man. Up to no good, he lived his ruthless life near Siena, Italy back in the late 1100s. But he is said to have had heavenly visions that affected him deeply and altered the course of his life.

As the tale goes, he met an angel on the road one day who confronted him about his lifestyle and told him he needed to give up his worldly ways. Guidotti couldn't fathom doing anything of the kind. He told the angel as much, saying the very idea of trying to reform him was a waste of effort, as far-fetched as trying to cut through stone with a sword.

To dramatize his point, he took his sword and struck the rock in front of him. His plan backfired, however, when instead of bouncing off the surface, the blade sliced through the stone as if it were butter, then stuck. Astonished and humbled, Guidotti spent the rest of his life as a dedicated Christian. His sword is still there to this day, hilt protruding from the rock, baffling scientists and fascinating tourists.

Whether or not the tale has any basis in history, I like what it suggests. Guidotti went into the conversation refusing to believe God's word could cut through his own cynicism. But the visual of a literal, physical sword piercing a rock opened his eyes and convinced him the sword of the Spirit had the power to achieve something equally miraculous within his soul.

Paul shared a similar conviction. The sword is the final element he mentions in his listing of the armor:

> Take up the helmet of salvation, and **the sword of the Spirit**, which is the word of God . . .

I discovered Bible quizzing at church camp one summer. I wasn't just good at it: I dominated the field of fifth grade competitors who didn't realize it was a blood sport.

The name of the game was speed, being the first one to recognize a verse and correctly identify where it came from in Scripture. While other campers used their free time swimming and running around like normal kids, I memorized the lists of verses ahead of each match. My strategy involved throwing my arms in the air when I jumped up to attract attention. And I always wore my bright yellow T-shirt with the big John Deere logo so I was readily visible to the judges.

I crammed a lot of Bible into my brain that way, with no interest at all in grappling with content. And I can't say much of it stuck with me beyond those heady days of glory.

For a long time, I looked back on that era with a bit of derision and disdain. It seemed a misguided way to generate interest in the written word of God, almost sacrilegious (not to mention more than a little nerdy). But now, I can hold the memory with more affection. It reminds me of young children sword fighting, serious about the fun while unconsciously growing muscle memory and coordination.

Through the camp experience, I inadvertently gained an ease and familiarity in navigating my way around the Old and New Testaments. And it injected an element of playfulness to something that is normally approached with such deadly earnestness.

It seems fitting for there to be an element of joy when we think of communication from our Father who loves us. But the gift of this piece of armor is often obscured by our complex history with it.

Scripture has never been easier to obtain. More than one hundred million Bibles are sold annually, with the average American owning three. Even those who don't possess one can readily find many of the eighty thousand translations free of charge online, instantly available on their computers and smartphones. There are countless formats and themed versions that tailor the text for every category of Christian.

The world is awash in Bibles. And yet biblical literacy is arguably at an all-time low. Fewer and fewer people actually read the endless copies being pumped out.

Sometimes, the lack of engagement with Scripture is deliberate. Stories that people absorbed easily when they were young now land differently on the ears and heart. Some passages sound unbelievable, while others strike us as offensive. One friend of mine went through a season where he couldn't read many verses without flashbacks to the preacher of his childhood who abused the authority of the Bible to ensure conformity. But he felt guilty for not wanting to have regular devotional time.

Such stories are all too common, creating enormous hurdles for countless believers. I encouraged my friend to give himself some grace and even take a break from force-feeding Scripture to himself. He has already ingested a great deal; the Holy Spirit didn't need to add new material to be at work in him.

> A word from the Lord is a powerful thing, and the temptation to abuse such power always proves strong.

It would be disrespectful of me to offer any easy responses to what has been such a painful topic for so many. Not all the problematic texts presented to us in Scripture can be explained away. But I do know that the Jesus who gave sight to the blind heals our eyes, too. He can even redeem his own Word, in a sense, causing it to speak to us in fresh and life-giving ways when we have had valid cause to dismiss it.

And we need it to speak, because we need a sword that we aren't afraid to pick up. It's vital to our existence.

Yet doing so should give us pause. Ever since Peter lopped off Malchus' ear in the Garden of Gethsemane, the Lord has been cleaning up the messes left by misguided disciples brandishing swords wantonly about. The world bears the scars from Christians who have weaponized the Bible down through the centuries. Untold damage has been done in the name of this piece of the armor.

The potential for destruction is understandable. A word from the Lord is a powerful thing, and the temptation to abuse such power always proves strong.

How can we take up the sword without wreaking havoc? How can we follow Paul's admonition to correctly handle the word of truth (2 Timothy 2:15)?

Theologians have argued over whether the Bible is the Word of God or if it *contains* the Word of God. It might be more helpful to reverse things and say *the Word of God contains the Bible*, rather than the other way around. God's Word—his expression of himself—is bigger than simply that which is written down. Christ, the eternal Word, existed with God in the very beginning, long before any original manuscripts of the Bible were composed (or lost).

The thirteenth chapter of Revelation tells us that not only was Christ in eternity past; *he was already slain*. That means the cross and God's salvation agenda predate creation. Therefore, the gospel— God's redeeming work on our behalf—came ahead of the Bible. To paraphrase P. T. Forsyth, the gospel was an action before it was in the pages of Scripture.

Christians routinely talk about the Bible having authority. But where does that authority reside? It is not located in the precision of the nouns and verbs chosen by the authors or in the claims Scripture makes about itself (important as those things may be). What makes the written word authoritative is that it speaks the message of the pre-existent Living Word.

After his resurrection, Jesus showed his disciples how all the Old Testament scriptures pointed to him. Every portion of the Law and the Prophets bears witness to the fact that he preceded the Bible, and he alone gives us its fullest meaning. That is not always apparent. At first glance, entire sections can leave us bored or alarmed. I must admit that long genealogies and stories of inexplicable violence continue to elude explanation for me.

Yet I have found repeatedly that even in obscure and troubling passages, Christ has met me when I consciously looked for him and waited for his arrival. He showed up in Esther advocating for her people. He became the ark in the river of my mind, holding back the waters. He rebuilt me alongside Nehemiah, and he shut the lion's mouths I was sure would tear me apart.

His presence has surprised me enough times and in enough texts that I am willing to entrust him with those I still don't understand. As Irenaeus wrote in the second century, "If anyone, therefore, reads the Scriptures with attention, he will find in them an account of Christ . . . For Christ is the treasure which was hid in the field . . . the treasure hid in the Scriptures is Christ."[28]

That's why Paul, great Torah scholar that he was, chose to know nothing except Jesus Christ crucified. There was no other secret to unearth. We have learned to handle the word of truth well when our use of it reveals the Savior and our need for him.

That might sound like an easier task with the New Testament, where Jesus is more obviously the main character. Yet we miss him there, too. Our attention is drawn to the instructional passages without seeing the grace underneath that gives them meaning.

We get ourselves into trouble with the sword of the Spirit when we forget that Scripture serves the gospel. No matter how much we profess our allegiance to the Bible, we're using it improperly when we promote our own agendas with it. We cause harm wielding it to maintain control over others. We swing it around too lightly when we treat it like a to-do list for holiness or a crystal ball to show us the future. And it is not a collection of charms to ward off evil or to unlock blessings.

> We get ourselves into trouble with the sword of the Spirit when we forget the Scripture serves the gospel.

Scripture's highest purpose is to communicate how God has reconciled us to himself through Christ. When we lose sight of that, we diminish the very text we claim to revere. Before we go about applying verses to life, we can ask one simple question: how does this passage take me back to Jesus and his cross?

We may still find many profound, worthwhile insights in the Bible without such a question. It is, after all, the Word that never returns void. But we rob the text of its force and center when we fail to connect it to Christ.

A second reality about the sword is that handling Scripture correctly does not mean gaining mastery over it. We envision ourselves putting in the time with the Bible to develop expert-level knowledge of it. Then we will feel in command, taking charge of how and when it is applied.

When I first became a pastor, I remember many times when I would start out at the beginning of a week eagerly looking forward to expounding on a chapter. Mondays would be full of confidence in what I was sure the text meant.

But by the middle of the week, I was in despair. The more I sat with the passage, the less clear it became. This happened so frequently that my wife began to refer to it as my "Wednesday fog." By the time I got up to preach on Sunday, my initial hubris was pounded out of me, and my interpretation looked far different than it had started out.

There are no "easy" portions of the Bible. Our relationship to God's Word will always be one of surrender, not control. Paul refers to it as the sword *of the Spirit*. It belongs to him and not to us. That means we can expect him to carry it far more than we do. And he always retains ownership.

When Paul wrote Ephesians, he chose a broad Greek term for sword that can refer to anything from a knife to a machete. The author of Hebrews uses the same term to describe God's Word, often translated into English as "double-edged sword." However, the Message version offers a different take that is enlightening:

Hebrews 4:12 (MSG)

His powerful Word is sharp as a surgeon's scalpel, cutting through everything, whether doubt or defense, laying us

open to listen and obey. Nothing and no one can resist
God's Word. We can't get away from it—no matter what.

In this interpretation, the Holy Spirit is the one with the blade in his hand, the Great Physician deftly applying the Word to work his healing.

As I navigated my meltdown, it took me several months to gain any clarity about what I was experiencing. But one deeply ingrained instinct that kicked in almost immediately was the impulse to reach for Scripture.

Looking back on that season now, it seems less as if I "took up" the sword and more as if I checked myself into the hospital with it. At the time, I didn't feel I had the strength to wield it with any skill. But I could surround myself with God's Word.

The Spirit went to work with his scalpel. And a shift began to happen inside me as I approached the Word from a different place. I was no longer a preacher looking for a sharable pearl, or even a studious disciple ready to learn. This was abject poverty. I was hungry and thirsty, and I gulped down Scripture like a dying man. Only God's truth and light could penetrate the cloud of confusion hanging over my head, the layers of doubt and defense Hebrews talks about.

Doubt and defense. Those are the reactions the enemy seeks to ignite in us with the flaming arrows discussed earlier. Scripture as a double-edged sword or scalpel becomes our best tool for cutting through his lies.

ATTACK	"You're not good enough for God."	
WITHOUT THE SWORD	**Doubt:** "Am I even acceptable?"	**Defense:** "I'm working hard to live right."
WITH THE SWORD	God loves me. John 3:16 No condemnation in Jesus. Romans 8:1 He is with me always. Matthew 28:20 My future is secure. 2 Corinthians 5:5	It's not about getting it right. Romans 4:6 God is my only rescue. Psalm 91:3 Christ offers me rest. Matthew 11:28 Christ came to help. Luke 5:32

ATTACK	"God's not good enough for you."	
WITHOUT THE SWORD	**Doubt:** "Can I trust God's heart?"	**Defense:** "I can find more than God offers."
WITH THE SWORD	God is the source of good. James 1:17 God loves giving to us. John 3:16 Everything is ours in Christ. Matthew 28:20 God has our interest at heart. 2 Corinthians 5:5	Chasing more never ends. Ecclesiastes 5:10 God's love is what satisfies. Psalm 90:14 God meets all my needs. Philippians 4:19 No one outloves Jesus. John 15:13

Jesus provided the supreme example for us of what it looks like in real life to fend off the enemy with the sword. In the fourth chapter of Matthew, his intense time of temptation in the desert brought assault after assault. Every argument the devil presented sounded reasonable and even desirable. And every time a new arrow flew, Jesus saw through the deception. He held his ground with Scripture, countering each lie by saying, "It is written . . ."

That singular strategy worked. Christ's inexhaustible familiarity with God's written word gave him exactly what he needed when he needed it. Truth punctured the inflated claims and showed how hollow they were. In the end, the enemy ran out of ammunition and fled. It was a decisive victory.

Still.

That was Jesus. And even in his case, the battle left him depleted. He expended a tremendous amount of energy in that fight, which leaves us wondering: if Christ, in all his wisdom, found it taxing to implement Scripture in his struggle, how can we possibly hope to hang on with our much more limited understanding and strength?

My grandfather was an asparagus farmer with a mechanical mind. No one would have accused him of being too bookish. Yet his love of the Bible ran deep, and he studied it faithfully. My dad recalls from childhood how Grandpa would sit by the stove in the morning, flipping through a thick stack of cards on which were different verses he had memorized. He reviewed them often to keep them fresh in his mind.

While in the hospital recovering from heart surgery, my grandfather experienced a stroke and ended up in a coma for two weeks. Most of those days remained shrouded in fog for the rest of his life, but he could vividly recall the sensation of horrifying darkness and being aware that he was desperately sick. Though his body was shut down, his mind reached for one of the many verses he had committed to memory. To his dismay, he could not recall a single one. All the years of diligently poring over Scripture were unable to help him in his greatest moment of crisis. The terror of the solitude was unbearable.

In a panic, he prayed for a sign. Like Thor calling for his hammer, he begged for even one word of Scripture to come to him. But he was met by nothing but a blank silence.

With his eyes, ears, and even his own mind incapable of supplying him with God's Word, he realized any comfort would have to come directly from God himself. And then at last, a voice spoke: "I will never leave thee, nor forsake thee." He could hardly fathom the relief that flooded over him. It was as if thick clouds parted. He clung to those words and repeated them to himself again and again.

Then more words arrived, unexpected words from Christ on the cross: "My God, my God, why hast Thou forsaken me?"

The contrast in the two statements moved him deeply. In his comatose state, my grandfather caught a glimpse of the separation Jesus suffered. His Savior understood the overwhelming and intolerable nature of his aloneness. There was a solidarity, a "withness" he hadn't recognized before. God's Word of promise to never leave took on far more personal meaning.

I find that story comforting. It speaks to a sword that remains living and active, even in times when our capacities to reach for it or wield it are impaired. God's Word has a will of its own, and it works on our behalf, independent of our control. There's more mercy in this weapon than we could ever imagine.

Deuteronomy 33:29a

Who is like you, a people saved by the Lord?
He is your shield and helper and your glorious sword.

FOR REFLECTION

1. What do you find most difficult about Bible reading?

2. How does it change things to search for Christ even in the Old Testament? What might be a challenge to that approach?

3. Can you think of a verse or passage that the Holy Spirit has used in your life to cut through doubt or defense?

ELEVEN

WITHNESS

It's so much more friendly with two.

A. A. Milne

Only equals make friends . . .

Maya Angelou

The assignment for my high school psychology class was straightforward: I had to ask friends and family for one word that described me. As I collected responses, most people gave the innocuous, unremarkable answers you'd expect, such as "funny" or "nice" or "talented."

Then I put the question to my father. He paused for a long moment, pen pressed to his lips as he contemplated his answer. Finally he looked at me and said, "Self-contained."

His choice of a hyphenated word pushed the bounds of the assignment, but it was the least predictable answer I'd received, so I heard him out. Dad went on to explain that he saw both positive and negative connotations in that term. I had the resources within me to accomplish things on my own. I was a world unto myself and could function well independently. Yet he could see it was going to be difficult for me to relate with people on more than a surface level if I couldn't be vulnerable.

Decades later, I marvel at how perceptive his concerns proved to be. I wish I had known how to take them to heart back then and cultivate more connectedness earlier in life. But at the time, I saw no downside to being self-contained. As far as I was concerned, the less help I needed, the better. I didn't want to be lonely, but I liked not having to rely on anyone else. I could always count on me.

> If the Spirit of Christ is within each of us, when we come together, we bring the presence of the Lord himself to one another.

Until I couldn't.

It's hard to be self-contained when you no longer trust what your own brain is telling you. Anxious desperation finally lowered my guard. In my broken-down state, I had to heed my friend Bill's encouragement to "press into relationship," which was the opposite of what came naturally in the moment. I wanted to retreat.

It was a foreign sensation to own my limits and let people in after years of fending for myself. But it humanized me in a way I hadn't known I'd been missing my entire adult life. In Ezekiel-like fashion, my fortress of a heart showed signs of melting back into flesh.

God knew what he was talking about when he said it wasn't good for us to be alone. We need one another. And that's a blessing—not a drawback. Just a few chapters before expounding on the armor of God, Paul reminded the Ephesians that God had given them a "glorious inheritance in his holy people" (Ephesians 1:18).

The gloriousness he describes differs from other communities of like-minded individuals. Church can and does provide the fellowship and support you'd expect from any healthy social network, but the source of it goes far deeper. If the Spirit of Christ is within each of us, when we come together, we bring the presence of the Lord himself to one another. Jesus said that where even two or three gather, he is right there in the midst (Matthew 18:20). The same word appears in Revelation when we're told he walks among the golden lampstands of his churches (Revelation 2:1).

Jesus occupies the between. Have you ever seen an arc of electrical current produced when two electrodes are in close proximity? A brilliant band of heat and light illuminates the gap. When followers of Jesus come together, the same Christ who indwells us individually also inhabits the space created between us where he can be seen. All the exchanges and actions and emotions that mark our connections generate opportunities for his character and work to be revealed. Christ's "withness" animates ours.

That may sound idealistic, since anyone who has been part of any church anywhere can tell you interactions between Christians are hardly all sweet and light. But even our brokenness cannot invalidate Jesus' claim to be present. Dietrich Bonhoeffer goes so far as to say that when there is misunderstanding and hurt between Christians, that in itself has a redemptive effect, because it prods us to remember our own fallen state and thank God for our shared forgiveness in Christ.[29]

The gift of the church and the gift of God's armor go hand in hand. It's much easier to wear the armor when we have someone else to help us step into it.

Paul told the Galatians, "Carry each other's burdens, and in this way you will fulfill the law of Christ" (Galatians 6:2). The law he's referring to, of course, is Christ's command for us to love one another as he loved us. That love shows up when we become armor bearers, helping to shoulder each other's heavy burdens in the middle of the fight.

How do we go about that? In Old Testament times, armor bearers carried the various pieces of weaponry and protective gear for their superior officers. They risked their lives to support others in the thick of battle.

During one of the many conflicts between Israel and the Philistines, Saul's army had been reduced to a mere six hundred troops, cornered by more than three thousand enemy soldiers. While the Israelites waited for a way out of their predicament, Jonathan, the king's son, took matters into his own hands.

1 Samuel 14:1–15

One day Jonathan son of Saul said to his young armor-bearer, "Come, let's go over to the Philistine outpost on the other side." But he did not tell his father.

Ordinarily, Jonathan and Saul shared each other's confidence. But because of the dangerous (some would say reckless) nature of Jonathan's idea to sneak into the enemy camp, he kept his plan private. The armor-bearer was the only exception, the lone companion Jonathan found safe enough to share his secret.

Given the brazen nature of what was being proposed and the threat it posed to his own life, the armor-bearer demonstrated remarkable poise as Jonathan spoke. His reaction showed no hint of disapproval or alarm. He didn't laugh or criticize or correct or run and tell Saul. His singular aim was to support Jonathan.

Withness means listening well. Have you ever found yourself in a conversation where midway through baring your soul, it becomes clear that the other person has checked out mentally? You recognize the vacant stare, the passive nods, the restless glancing around. At some point along the way, the listener stopped being attentive. They are no longer with you.

I can read these telltale signals because I have sent them too often myself. Many times, I'm so eager to share my own thoughts and opinions that I begin formulating my reply before the other person has even finished talking. Or I drift into a preoccupied state where I'm biding my time until I can exit the conversation. If I'm not fully listening, I cannot be meaningfully with you.

In his book, *Caring Enough to Hear and Be Heard*, David Augsburger writes, "Being heard is so close to being loved that for the average person, they are almost indistinguishable."[30]

We tend to doubt the power in such a simple act as hearing someone out. We're convinced that the real impact will result from what we say back by way of consolation or advice. When Job's three friends first heard about his suffering, their best ministry happened in the week they spent sitting at his side, not saying a word. It was only after they opened up their mouths to speak that the bad theology began to flow. When there are many words, Proverbs says, sin is sure to show up (Proverbs 10:19).

My first forays into pastoral counseling and visitation filled me with intense stress. Internally, I felt enormous pressure to know the exact words to share in each crisis. Talking on the fly is not my strength. What if I froze or drew a blank? How could I possibly come up with the right thing to say when someone was looking to me for comfort or wisdom?

I soon found my fears to be completely misplaced. No one in crisis needed my words. They needed my ears. And my presence—my attentive, physical withness. In fact, the more acute the crisis and the more intense the pain, the less I needed to speak. When words were called for, the ones most appreciated typically came in the form of empathy ("I'm so sorry"), validation ("That makes sense"), or curiosity ("Tell me more about that"). Those types of responses center around listening to the other person, not solving a problem.

> No one in crisis needed my words. They needed my ears.

Jonathan's armor-bearer went beyond merely allowing him to speak:

> *"Do all that you have in mind," his armor-bearer said. "Go ahead; I am with you heart and soul."*

The odds of success were not good. Jonathan's plan was fraught with peril. But he was not going to be alone in the struggle. The armor-bearer declared his personal, costly commitment to stand at his side.

Withness enters the other person's fight. There's no indication that the armor-bearer felt any compelling personal need to take on the Philistines. He may not have related at all to Jonathan's strong impulse to start a confrontation. But it didn't matter. He made himself fully available for the sake of his relationship with Jonathan. That was his priority.

It's difficult to support someone else when we're questioning the validity of their battle. Our own limited experience may lead us to dismiss their struggle as exaggerated. We assume our lives represent the norm for everyone, so what comes easily to us should for them as well.

Our suspicious minds would do well to heed Margo McCaffery's insightful words to doctors and nurses when she wrote, "Pain is whatever the experiencing person says it is."[31] If someone describes their discomfort level as being at a ten, no outside observer can disagree and tell them it's only a four. We have to take them at their word.

Back in seminary, two professors greatly enhanced my understanding of this concept. They lived in different cities and taught at different schools that were thousands of miles apart. Yet since they were both Black, their theology shared a consciousness regarding race that was brand new to me. They had both encountered barriers within Christendom due to the color of their skin, and they recognized discrimination in places where I assumed a shared commitment to Christ would have resulted in greater equality.

Initially, my brain did not know how to process these new perspectives. Growing up as a white male in the suburbs of the

Pacific Northwest, I had rarely given a second thought to my own skin color, let alone its relationship to my faith. The world I grew up in gave me no cause to do so. My self-image was largely colorless, which I assumed made my outlook the more unbiased one. I resisted what my professors were saying because I didn't like what it suggested about my own unawareness. I didn't want my idealized view of the church at large to be challenged.

But pain is what the experiencing person says it is, not what a naïve student would like it to be. As these two godly men shared their life stories, stories marked by suffering and injustice, it was evident that the fact of how society responded to their Blackness shaped everything for them. Their senses were tuned in to all the subtle (and not-so-subtle) ways they were treated differently, simply because they were Black men.

My ability to remain unconscious of my color wasn't a marker of greater objectivity—it was a luxury I enjoyed as a member of a majority culture. I hadn't caused it or chosen it, but I did have a choice when it came to acknowledging the reality. The more I listened to my professors, the less I could remain in my own blindness and naïveté.

Even in acknowledging another person's truth, we can feel a strong urge to distance ourselves from it. We don't want to be associated with anything so ugly. We defend ourselves and conclude, "I'm not the one who did anything. It's not my problem."

Wouldn't the assertion that it's *not* my problem be precisely the meaning of carrying someone else's burden? As a Christian, am I not being asked to attend to the suffering of my fellow believers—

suffering that I might not feel so heavily myself? Otherwise, I'm just shouldering the load that matters to me personally.

And we cannot set about finding fault with people when the way in which they cry for help makes us uncomfortable. Imagine visiting someone in a hospital and unknowingly standing on their oxygen tube. If they begin slapping your arm to indicate something is wrong, you don't focus on how they're hurting you or accuse them of overreacting. Instead of becoming indignant, you move your feet.

> Even in acknowledging another person's truth, we can feel a strong urge to distance ourselves from it.

Witness isn't just for when it's convenient. Back in the third century, a professional actor came to faith in Christ, and it created a dilemma for him and his church. At that time, the church considered the world of theater blatantly immoral and tied to idolatry, and therefore incompatible with Christianity. The man asked the elders of his congregation if teaching acting might be an acceptable option for him, since he had no marketable skills besides stagecraft.

The elders came to the conclusion that if it was wrong for a Christian to act, then it would be equally wrong to teach the craft to others. However, they wanted to obtain a more official opinion, so they consulted with Cyprian, the bishop of neighboring Carthage.

Cyprian agreed that giving acting lessons was no different from performing. If one was offensive, so was the other. But the bishop told the church that since they were asking this man to give up his employment, they needed to be the ones to feed and clothe him. And then he went further: he said if their church was too small to afford that, they could send the actor to his church, and they would take care of his needs.

Cyprian sets a high bar for us when it comes to grasping our call to bear one another's burdens. It's far easier to hold to our moral high ground and let the other person work out for themselves how to muddle through on their own. We insist on viewing ourselves as separate from "the other" so we can be absolved of any responsibility. Yet Christ himself bore the ultimate other by entering into our struggle with sin that was completely foreign to him. That is where his withness shines. Surely, as Isaiah said, he took up *our* infirmities and carried *our* sorrows when they were not his.

Of course, there's a potential danger in talk of carrying one another's burdens. Anne Lamott once said help is the sunny side of control. We readily overstep to take on responsibility that is not ours. We can think we have such clarity about someone else's problem that we jump into fixing mode. Once again, Jonathan's armor-bearer sheds an instructive light for us:

> *Jonathan climbed up, using his hands and feet, with his armor-bearer right behind him. The Philistines fell before Jonathan, and his armor-bearer followed and killed behind him. In that first attack Jonathan and his armor-bearer killed some twenty men in an area of about half an acre.*

The fighting was fierce, and Jonathan demonstrated impressive skill against such a large band of warriors. But he couldn't take on all the threats at once, and some slipped past him. Perhaps he could not see them. He may have been preoccupied with what was right in front of him. The further he advanced, the more Philistines were able to move to attack from behind. But the armor-bearer was right there, guarding his back.

Withness looks out for what is being missed. As we have seen in the previous chapters, the armor of God consists entirely of God's grace and our full confidence in the work of the cross. Our battles are the times we are most likely to forget what God has already done, because so much seems to be riding on us. That means that to be armor-bearers, our job is less about taking over someone else's battle and more about carrying the grace of God into their life that they might miss when they are in the thick of the fight. Our role becomes less about solving and more about communicating love that's hard to see when you're struggling.

When my anxiety is at its most spun up, one way it presents itself is through an intense compulsion to confess or explain myself. The more I attempt to give voice to what I am thinking and feeling, the greater the sense of panic that the words are inadequate.

Relief came in a conversation with a counselor. Into my frantic disquiet, he introduced a new image. He helped me picture Christ meeting me even as I tried to speak. I could see him reaching a hand to touch my mouth as if to say, "That's enough."

Such a simple thought of Jesus was powerful enough to calm my mind and body back down. It was as if the seraph who applied the coal from the fire to the lips of the prophet was now telling me I could rest. It was exactly what I needed. But I wouldn't have envisioned that idea on my own. In the throes of my struggle, the belt of truth had loosened and slipped. It took a friend entering the fight with me to help me retighten it.

It is easy, especially for those in helping professions, to only think of withness in terms of how we come alongside someone else. Yet we need to be open to what they bring our way as well.

Many years ago, I took an evening class that was, by and large, unmemorable. I cannot recall the content of the lectures, but a single conversation has remained with me.

Most students in the class were young white males in pursuit of a pastoral career. One Korean woman sat in the back every week, listening. She spoke little, and when she did, her strong accent made her difficult to understand. To my shame, I quickly dismissed her as someone who had little to contribute.

Then a session came when discussion turned to the topic of persecution. One by one, future preachers all eagerly shared their opinions on the entire concept of suffering for our faith. After this had gone on for a while, the Korean student unexpectedly joined in. "I grew up in a Buddhist family in Korea," she said. "I became a Christian, and every Sunday as I walked home from church, I knew that when I arrived my father would beat me for going to the service."

The rest of us sat in stunned silence, feeling humbled to be in this sister's presence. Every comment from the previous half hour now sounded embarrassingly shallow. I had arrogantly written her off as if she didn't matter. Yet her life proved to be the lesson I needed most.

We are not fully with others if we don't engage them as equals, capable of showing us more of what it means to be human and more of the God in whose image they were created. Watchman Nee wrote, "Fellowship means, among other things, that we are ready to receive of Christ from others. Other believers minister Christ to me, and I am ready to receive."[32]

Throughout the entire story with Jonathan, we never learn the armor-bearer's name, which seems fitting. Armor-bearing isn't an activity that draws attention to itself; it's about support for someone else, in the belief that God is doing something big.

And he is doing big things. As Jonathan aptly said, whether through few or many, God does his work. Can we come alongside each other to be a part of it, and to say, "I am with you heart and soul"?

FOR REFLECTION

1. Who do you think of as the best example of someone being with you in your struggles? What makes them stand out?

2. Do you find yourself dismissing people's problems as not your own, getting too involved in trying to fix them, or getting too fixated on your ideas about what they need? How do we know what is ours to do?

3. What about listening feels difficult? What is one way you could intentionally expand your skills as a listener?

TWELVE

THE LAST WORD

Listen, my friend! Your helplessness
is your best prayer.

Ole Hallesby

When I pray, coincidences happen,
and when I don't, they don't.

William Temple, Archbishop of Canterbury

It's standard Hollywood fare: the hero walks into a supplier's shop to gear up for the final showdown in the movie. A wide array of technology and/or firepower is paraded out for consideration. Overall, it's an impressive display of strength, but one question invariably follows: "What else do you have?"

At that point, the shopkeeper disappears into the back room and returns with one more special option—a secret resource in a league of its own, with the extra ingredient necessary to get the job done.

We have now seen all that Paul has to show us in terms of the armor of God. Every component has been named and made available to us. But there is one weapon still remaining in Paul's arsenal, one essential element for when we're under attack. In the verses that follow, he shows how to use it.

Ephesians 6:18
And pray in the Spirit on all occasions with all kinds of prayers and requests. With this in mind, be alert and always keep on praying for all the Lord's people.

Pray, says Paul. Always, and for everyone. He gives the impression that he's not particular as to the mechanics, so long as we sustain the habit. Prayer, like the armor, keeps our faith breathing.

Yet discussing the topic of prayer tends to drain us. Because when we're told to pray, we immediately recognize the thinness of our own prayer life, either in quantity or quality. We're convinced we should be praying more. We don't think there's enough substance in our words. We hate admitting we only go to God when we're asking for something. And we feel sheepish about talking to him out loud where others can evaluate us.

How can a spiritual activity that promises such blessing generate so much insecurity?

This is nothing new about prayer. Back in 1626, John Donne preached a sermon in which he made this honest confession that still resonates:

I throw myself down in my chamber, and I call in, and invite God, and his angels thither, and when they are there, I neglect God and his angels for the noise of a fly, for the rattling of a coach, for the whining of a door; I talk on in the same posture of praying, eyes lifted up, knees bowed down, as though I prayed to God; and if God or his angels should ask me when I thought last of God in that prayer, I cannot tell. Sometimes I find that I had forgot what I was about, but when I began to forget it I cannot tell. A memory of yesterday's pleasures, a fear of tomorrow's dangers, a straw under my knee, a noise in mine ear, a light in mine eye, an anything, a nothing, a fancy, a chimera in my brain troubles me in my prayer.[33]

Discomfort and discouragement in prayer run through the Bible as well. The Israelites were so self-conscious they begged Moses to do all the praying on their behalf. Jesus noted how pagans babbled on and on in their prayers. Pharisees tried to sound impressive. The disciples fell asleep. Paul summed things up well when he wrote, "We do not know what we ought to pray for" (Romans 8:26).

My father was an avid gardener when I was young, and every spring we would hitch up the trailer to the back of our VW bus and head to the farm up the street, where we would acquire a fresh load of cattle manure to mix into the soil.

While Dad set about shoveling, my sister and I would go on grand adventures exploring the pasture. One time we set out further than ever before across the lower fields, climbing through a fence and into the nearby woods.

I had not gone far into the trees when I stepped into deep mud and could not move. My feet began to sink, and panic began to set in. When I strained to dislodge myself, my boot stayed stuck while my foot came free. I turned and ran back to the fence. Somehow, I had missed the fact that it was electric, and as I grabbed the wire, a tremendous shock ripped through my body.

At that point I gave a terrified shriek and began crying. But when I looked up, I saw my dad, running over the top of the hill toward me, faster than I had ever seen him move before.

> Desperation has a way of helping us move past our own sense of inadequacy in prayer.

Even in my inarticulate state, when I had gotten myself in a place I didn't belong, he was there to comfort me the moment I called out.

That's the picture of prayer that stays with me. The specifics of form and content take a back seat to the assurance that we have a Father whose heart is for us and always ready to respond.

Desperation has a way of helping us move past our own sense of inadequacy in prayer. It often ends up being our doorway into honest communion with God. Oswald Chambers said, "We do not pray at all until we are at our wits' end."[34]

Wits' end is precisely where anxiety took me. Prayer grew to become my lifeline even as it shrunk to the very basics in my practice. For months, I cycled through the first thirty Psalms again and again. Just one per day, and at the end of the month I started over. That small collection of Psalms became my prayer book. We tend to assume quantity is always better with Scripture, but the repetition of narrow portions held me together.

The thirteenth Psalm gave voice to my fears over how long I would be battling my thoughts. Psalm eighteen helped me picture God's powerful response, even his anger, over the distress I was experiencing. And when my urgency became unbearable, Psalm twenty-seven called me to wait on God.

These Bible prayers became my prayers. When I didn't have confidence in my own words, God graciously supplied his words for me.

This is the beauty Paul would have us see: we're not praying alone. His first encouragement to us in this passage is to pray in the Spirit. We have the Spirit of Christ himself praying with and for us.

Romans 8:26–27

In the same way, the Spirit helps us in our weakness. We do not know what we ought to pray for, but the Spirit himself intercedes for us through wordless groans. And he who searches our hearts knows the mind of the Spirit, because the Spirit intercedes for God's people in accordance with the will of God.

Our lack of expertise in prayer doesn't spell the end of its effectiveness. God was never asking for that in the first place. Christ's own Spirit takes all our stumbling, overwrought pleas and distills them into powerful connection with our Father.

I lose sight of this truth on a regular basis and operate as if my prayers are as self-contained as I am. I strive to forge "good" prayers that are worthy of being heard. A gnawing self-doubt can leave me wondering if I've poured enough time and energy into my supplications to warrant a response.

It is a tremendous relief to remember that God's redeeming work extends even to our prayers. Their acceptability rides on his shoulders, not ours. Just a few verses further in the same chapter, Paul reinforces his point that we have an advocate:

Romans 8:34

Who then is the one who condemns? No one. Christ Jesus who died—more than that, who was raised to life—is at the right hand of God and is also interceding for us.

Scripture doubles down on this, assuring us that Jesus lives to pray for us constantly (Hebrews 7:25). There is no break in his relationship with God, and therefore no point at which our feeble prayers have to stand on their own. Our faith is in the one who prays for us.

> God as the perfect parent knows better than anyone that his children are far from the same.

This could lead someone to ask, "Why pray at all, then? If Jesus is doing the perfect praying already, what good is bothering with it on our end?"

Such logic misconstrues the relationship. Imagine if, while growing up, you had reasoned, "My mom's cooking dinner. Why should I come to the table?" Meal prep isn't the issue. Not showing up for dinner wouldn't have lessened your responsibility. You would have simply been depriving yourself of Mom's cooking (and taking yourself out of community).

The mystery of prayer doesn't depend on our efforts, but it is what feeds us. Jesus told his disciples he had food they knew nothing about (John 4:32). He was referring to his communion with his Father, and he regularly spent time stealing away to recharge his soul. Our spirits wither inside for lack of prayer.

Those times with God offer great roominess in terms of what they look like. Paul tells us to *pray on all occasions, with all kinds of prayers and requests.* There is no wrong time to pray, and there is no wrong subject to pray about.

I have three grown children who are distinctly unlike each other. My wife and I are often amazed that such diversity in personality and gifting came from the same household. Whenever we tried following a uniform parenting plan for all three, it never worked. We learned we needed to communicate with each of them individually and in their own, beautifully unique ways.

God as the perfect parent knows better than anyone that his children are far from the same. It stands to reason, then, that prayer itself will take on a myriad of forms reflecting the variety within the family.

If you grew up in a rigid religious environment with tight expectations around how to pray, breaking out of old narratives may mean finding entirely new ways to conceptualize a conversation with God. Taking a nature walk, journaling, or being alone with God in the car might serve better for hearing from him than kneeling in a sanctuary.

Some Christians are wary of contemplative approaches such as centering prayer, which relies on silence more than words to commune with God. Yet many with anxiety have found those ancient practices to be a tremendous lifeline and deeply restorative.

I have friends who are very enthusiastic about certain prayer rhythms that I personally find too prescriptive. But to paraphrase Paul, what does it matter which tool opens the door to more prayer? God can meet us in so many ways. Whatever enables someone to stay in (or return to) authentic communication with him is a worthy vehicle. Because of them, we can rejoice.

People in Scripture used anything as a good excuse to pray. They prayed about big things like battles and plagues. But they also prayed for very relatable human needs. They prayed to find a spouse. They prayed to have children. They prayed for parenting wisdom. They prayed for health and safety and the weather. They prayed when they were in trouble. They prayed when they were hungry. They prayed about work. They prayed when they were grateful, when they were down, when they were worried, when they were mad, when they were alone, and when they were with a group. They prayed over their plans and when they didn't have any.

They prayed standing up. They prayed facing a wall. They prayed looking out the window. They prayed on their knees. They prayed with hands in the air. They wrote prayers. They made up songs with them. We can take from their experience that there's no circumstance under which praying is out of place. The Benedictine monk, Luigi Gioia, notes how even something as basic as our negative emotions can serve as a prompt for prayer. "When I start praying, I just focus on what is the dominant feeling in my heart," he says. "If it is a positive feeling, like joy, I offer this joy to the Lord. If it is a negative feeling, like frustration or tiredness,

I start from there and I say to the Lord, 'Lord, I'm tired' or 'I'm frustrated.'"[35]

It is easy to postpone prayer in those situations with the awareness that we're not currently "in the Spirit." We don't feel thankful. We don't feel trusting. And because of that, we don't want to pray and be hypocritical. We decide we'll wait until we're inspired or in a better place mentally.

> Praise doesn't depend on my current state of mind in order to be true.

No one wants to simply go through the motions. But sometimes motion is what's needed. Rote prayer can be the very thing that leads us to heartfelt prayer. If we wait for the right moment or feeling, it will never arrive. It will not hurt the outcome for your prayer to start out feeling forced or unnatural.

We are never being fake when we declare who God is. Praise doesn't depend on my current state of mind in order to be true. I can boldly say God is gracious and holy and kind and good, letting the reality of his character draw me in even as I utter the words. Proclaiming what we know in the face of what we feel can be a powerful way of countering the enemy's lie that we have to be in a certain headspace to pray.

Brother Gioia's practice of connecting even mundane experiences and feelings to prayer frees him from overthinking how he approaches God. He has a memorable rule of thumb for his prayer life: "Keep it simple. Keep it honest. Keep it going."[36]

It isn't as though God needs us to inform him about our life. He already knows exactly where we are on every level. Expressing ourselves through prayer realigns our own thinking. As we place our desires and concerns before him, we begin to see them differently, and we find ourselves changing in his presence. There is an unburdening inside as we consciously turn over our cares to his keeping.

Prayer changes our relationship to other people.

Prayer also takes us outside of ourselves, because Paul says we are to *keep on praying for all the saints*. By saints he means our fellow believers. Prayer changes our relationship to other people. Interceding for someone regularly cannot help but soften our attitude.

Even more than that, in ways we don't begin to understand, our prayers are impactful in the lives of others. God may not need us in order to accomplish his work, but he still responds to our prayers on behalf of one another. He has chosen to include us in carrying out his will and furthering his kingdom. It is staggering to know that the God of the entire universe listens to us and gives consideration when we cry out for his intervention.

We can follow the example of Christ in knowing what to pray for one another. The book of John provides us with a glimpse of how Jesus prayed for his followers and what mattered most in his mind.

PRAYING FOR THE SAINTS

Themes we can borrow from Jesus' prayer in John 17

Spiritual Protection	"... protect them from the evil one." (v. 15)
Internal Joy	"... that they may have the full measure of my joy ..." (v. 13)
Personal Growth	"Sanctify them by the truth ..." (v. 17)
Relational Unity	"... that all of them may be one ..." (v. 21)
Global Witness	"Then the world will know ..." (v. 23)
Knowledge of God	"I ... will continue to make you known ..." (v. 26)

We have in this prayer much more than the parting wishes of a rabbi on behalf of his band of disciples. Jesus stated specifically that he prayed these words with all of his future followers in mind. This passage reflects his will for us. That means that we in turn can ask these same things for one another and have confidence that God cares about them as well.

In the wake of my struggles with anxiety, I've come to think differently about how I pray, whether I'm talking to God on behalf of others or myself. Eradication of suffering no longer seems the ultimate answer I'm seeking. As nice as that idea might be, my faith is no longer crushed when God doesn't take hardship out of the picture. P. T. Forsyth once wrote, "It is a greater thing to pray for pain's conversion than for its removal. It is more of grace to pray that God would make a sacrament of it."[37]

A sacrament. Could the very thing that I hated and fought for so long become a vehicle for experiencing more grace? Could God turn my fear and uncertainty into a means of growing my faith?

My prayers for my basal ganglia have changed. Instead of focusing all my pleas on some kind of miraculous healing (which I still wouldn't mind), I am learning to say, "Meet me in this. Take it and do whatever will help my faith grow."

It is a harder prayer to pray in many ways. Not because it requires more exertion, but because it means letting go of what I thought I wanted most. Harder, because it means facing realities. And harder because it means accepting what God provides and trusting his goodness.

> Could the very thing that I hated and fought for so long become a vehicle for experiencing more grace?

But prayer has always been hard work. Abraham negotiated in it. Jacob fought. Moses argued. Esther fasted. Hannah cried. Epaphras wrestled. Paul labored. And Jesus sweat blood. He lives, Hebrews says, to intercede for us, staying at our side in the task, infusing us with both strength and joy in it.

"Not my will, but yours be done." It is that garden prayer that changes everything, where Jesus does battle for us, encompassing our prayers with his own.

In the night of weary souls,
when courage and color
have been drained away
and my once willing spirit
has given way to fear
and my broken mind
refuses to respond
and my weakened body
cannot stay awake
in the desperate hour
and the fatigue
outweighs my intentions
and my intentions
are less than pure
and I am no help to myself—
in that place I find Christ,
praying for me.

Hallelujah.

FOR REFLECTION

1. Try a form of prayer that is outside your normal routine. What, if anything, came up that felt new or different as you tried it?

2. If Christ is praying for you, what do you hope is the content? Talk to him about that.

3. Who is on your mind that you can bring before the Lord? Use the "Praying for the Saints" chart as a guide.

ACKNOWLEDGMENTS

I always tell people I am a slow roast, and this book has borne that out. It has taken its own sweet time coming into the world and would not have made it at all without the shaping influence and encouragement of many people.

First off, thank you, Mom and Dad. Your love and faith form the backbone of my story and I'm so thankful for you both. My siblings, Jana and Jordan—you're right there with them. And I feel incredibly blessed to have the in-laws and extended family that I do. Love you all.

To New Day Church: I'm thanking you en masse because I can't list everyone by name. I hope you will still take my gratitude personally! You walked with me through every stage of this book's development and have painted such a refreshingly different picture for me of what church life can look like.

Isaiah—your response to my story made writing it down feel worth it.

I have had some gifted therapists who have helped me beyond measure along the way: Dr. David Waller, Dr. Ian Osborn, and, of course, my friend/counselor Bill Bedell. I can't even begin, buddy. Thank you all for caring so well for me.

I will be forever grateful to Lynnette Pennings and the team at Tyndale/Aspire for seeing potential in this book and championing it into existence. Kay Ben-Avraham's insightful editing refined the message immensely. The errors that remain are completely on me.

Thanks to my delightful grown-up kids, Isaac, Addison and Annika, who make the world a much better place. I love you all and am so proud of who you are.

Lastly, to my beautiful wife, Karin. You believed in this book before it existed and understood more than I did why my soul needed it to be written.

NOTES

CHAPTER 1 – MEET LEO

1   á Kempis, Thomas. *Of the Imitation of Christ: Four Books.* Boston: Lee & Shephard, 1871, 2.

2   Cox, Matthew. "Combat Engineer Receives Helmet that Saved His Life in Afghanistan." Posted April 20, 2016. *Military.com.* https://www.google.com/amp/s/www.military.com/daily-news/2016/04/20/combat-engineer-receives-helmet-that-saved-his-life-afghanistan.html/amp.

CHAPTER 2 – A STRONGER STRONG

3   Muncil, Tracy. "AWVI 2020 Survey: 1 in 3 US Adults Embrace Salvation through Jesus; More Believe It Can Be Earned." Posted August 4, 2020. *Cultural Research Center, Arizona Christian University.* https://www.arizonachristian.edu/2020/08/04/1-in-3-us-adults-embrace-salvation-through-jesus-more-believe-it-can-be-earned/.

4   Yancey, Phillip. "What's So Amazing About Grace?" Posted June 18, 2021. Video Bible Study, Session 1. *HarperChristian Resources.* https://www.youtube.com/watch?v=HA-YeA_I9rA&t=126s.

CHAPTER 3 – CONSCIENTIOUS OBJECTIONS

5   Bunyan, John. *The Work of Jesus Christ as an Advocate.* London: Dorman Newman, 1689, 115.

6   Kierkegaard, Søren. *The Concept of Dread.* Princeton: Princeton University Press, 1946, 142.

CHAPTER 4 – THE ARMOR OF ME

7   Forsyth, P. T. *Positive Preaching and the Modern Mind.* Carlisle, England: Paternoster Press, 1988, 165.

8   Osborn, Ian. *Can Christianity Cure Obsessive-Compulsive Disorder? A Psychiatrist Explores the Role of Faith in Treatment.* Grand Rapids, MI: Brazos Press, 2008, 91–108.

9   Martin, Thérèse. *St. Thérèse of Lisieux: Her Last Conversations.* Washington, D.C.: ICS Publications, 1977, 140.

10   Luther, Martin. "Commentary on St. Paul's Epistle to the Galatians." *Christian Classics Ethereal Library.* Online edition. https://www.ccel.org/ccel/luther/galatians.html.

11   Mellody, Pia. *Facing Codependence: What It Is, Where It Comes from, How It Sabotages Our Lives.* San Francisco: Harper Collins, 2003, 63.

12   Lewis, C. S. "On Writing for Children." *On Stories: And Other Essays on Literature.* New York: Harcourt Brace Jovanovich, 1982, 34.

13   Cloud, Henry and John Townsend. *Boundaries with Kids: How Healthy Choices Grow Healthy Children.* Grand Rapids, MI: Zondervan, 2001, 72.

CHAPTER 5 – TRUTH THAT SURROUNDS

14   Potok, Chaim. *The Promise.* New York: Anchor Books, 2005, 62.

15   "UMass Amherst Researcher Finds Most People Lie in Everyday Conversation." Posted June 10, 2002. *UMass Amherst Office of News & Media Relations.* https://www.umass.edu/archivenewsoffice/article/umass-amherst-researcher-finds-most-people-lie-everyday-conversation.

16   Mann, Heather, et al. "Cut from the Same Cloth: Similarly Dishonest Individuals Across Countries." *Journal of Cross-Cultural Psychology 46*, no. 6 (May 2016): 858–874.

17 Lake, Frank. *Clinical Theology: A Theological and Psychiatric Basis to Clinical Pastoral Care*. London: Darton, Longman & Todd, Ltd., 1966, 24–25.

18 Ralph Bunche as quoted in Riegel, Deborah Grayson and Ellen Dowling. *Tips of the Tongue: The Nonnative English Speaker's Guide to Mastering Public Speaking*. Oceanside, CA: Indie Books International, 2017, 2.

CHAPTER 6 – THE SECOND LIST LIFE

19 Forsyth, P. T. "The Problem of Forgiveness in the Lord's Prayer." In *The Sermon on the Mount: A Practical Exposition of the Lord's Prayer*, edited by E. Griffith-Jones, et al. Manchester, England: James Robinson, 1903, 190–191.

20 Beattie, Melody. "Acting As If." Posted July 2, 2020. *MelodyBeattie.com*. https://melodybeattie.com/acting-as-if/

CHAPTER 7 – SHOD

21 Koyama, Kosuke. *Three Mile an Hour God*. New York: Orbis Books, 1979, 7.

22 Moore, Russell. "My Dad Taught Me How to Love the Exvangelical." Posted October 21, 2021. *Christianity Today*. https://www.christianitytoday.com/ct/2021/october-web-only/russell-moore-dad-taught-love-exvangelical-pastor-church.html.

CHAPTER 8 – SHIELDS UP

23 Ryan, Juanita. "What I Learned While Our Son Was Still Using Drugs." *The National Association for Christian Recovery*. https://www.nacr.org/families/parents/what-i-learned-while-our-son-was-still-using-drugs.

24 Weil, Simone. *Simone Weil: An Anthology*. Edited by Siân Miles. New York: Grove Press, 2000, 202.

CHAPTER 9 – PRAYING FOR MY BASAL GANGLIA

25   Osborn, *Can Christianity*, 120.

26   Frohlich, Joel. "What Is Obsessive Compulsive Disorder?" Posted February 20, 2017. *Psychology Today*. https://www. psychologytoday.com/us/blog/consciousness-self-organization-and-neuroscience/201702/what-is-obsessive-compulsive-disorder.

27   Purdon, Christine and David Clark. *Overcoming Obsessive Thoughts: How to Gain Control of Your OCD*. Oakland, CA: New Harbinger Publications, 2005, 20.

CHAPTER 10 – THE SECRET TO SWORD FIGHTING

28   Irenaeus. *The Writings of Irenaeus, Volume 1*. Translated by Alexander Roberts and W. H. Rambaut. Edinburgh: T. & T. Clark, 1884.

CHAPTER 11 – WITHNESS

29   Bonhoeffer, Dietrich. *Life Together*. San Francisco: HarperCollins Publishers, 1954, 28.

30   Augsburger, David. *Caring Enough to Hear and Be Heard*. Ventura, CA: Regal Books, 1982, 12.

31   McCaffery, Margo. *Nursing Practice Theories Related to Cognition, Bodily Pain, and Man-Environment Interactions*. Los Angeles: UCLA Students Store, 1968, 8.

32   Nee, Watchman. *Changed into His Likeness*. Fort Washington, PA: CLC Publications, 2007, 104.

CHAPTER 12 – THE LAST WORD

33   Donne, John. *John Donne: The Major Works*. Edited by John Carey. New York: Oxford University Press, 1990, 373–374.

34   Chambers, Oswald. *Baffled to Fight Better: Job and the Problem of Suffering*. Grand Rapids, MI: Discovery House Publishers, 1990, 72.

35   Gioia, Luigi. "Why and How Should We Pray?" Alpha Film Series. Episode 5. Posted May 30, 2020. https://youtu.be/waIL-WeDW4k.

36   Gioia. "Why and How Should We Pray?"

37   Forsyth, P. T. *The Soul of Prayer.* Vancouver: Regent College Publishing, 1995, 47.

ABOUT THE AUTHOR

J. D. Peabody has always loved stories, and his career has been spent improving his ability to write and tell them. For nearly two decades, he wrote in the context of advertising and public relations agencies, where he gained an appreciation (or at least a tolerance) for being edited. He then switched fields entirely, attending seminary, helping start a new church and learning the discipline of writing for weekly sermon deadlines.

Along the way, he tried his hand at writing poetry and song lyrics, which met with some success and taught him the difference between connecting emotionally and just being clever with words. He published articles that required attention to word count. He also wrote multiple screenplays that honed his sense of dialogue and plot development.

J. D. is a native of the Pacific Northwest, where he lives with his wife, who offsets the perpetually gray skies.

Perfectly Suited is his first book for grown-ups. He is also the author of the children's novel, *The Inkwell Chronicles: The Ink of Elspet*.

Learn more about J. D. and his books at
www.jdpeabody.com